ONE PERCENT BETTER

ONE PERCENT BETTER

A New Business Process for Efficiency, Culture, and Innovation

JERRY C. PYKIET

JONES MEDIA
PUBLISHING

Jones Media Publishing
10645 N. Tatum Blvd. Ste. 200-166
Phoenix, AZ 85028
JonesMediaPublishing.com

Printed in the United States of America

ISBN: 978-1-948382-92-2 paperback

Disclaimer:

The characters and events portrayed in this book are fictitious. Any similarity to real persons, living or dead, is coincidental and not intended by the author.

TABLE OF CONTENTS

Introduction

In the 1590s, Galileo became a consultant for the Venetian arsenal, advising engineers and toolmakers, and helping to solve the biggest shipbuilding problems. He was largely responsible for creating major innovations in the production and logistics of shipbuilding.

Galileo's involvement in shipbuilding wasn't just about solving immediate technical issues; it was about revolutionizing the entire process. He introduced new methods and tools that improved efficiency and reduced costs, setting the stage for modern shipbuilding practices. His innovative approach allowed for faster production times and more reliable ships, which was crucial for trade and military purposes.

The Venetian arsenal was the first documented assembly line. Instead of building a boat for battle on dry land in one big building, they utilized Mother Nature's natural conveyor system, the flow of water going down a river. They figured out that they could take the total process of building the boat and divide it up into one day of work at each docking location. At the end of each day, they would move each boat to its next building station. After eight or ten docking stations, they would have a completed ship ready for battle. This was revolutionary because their competition would take a month or more to build a boat, and they completed one every day.

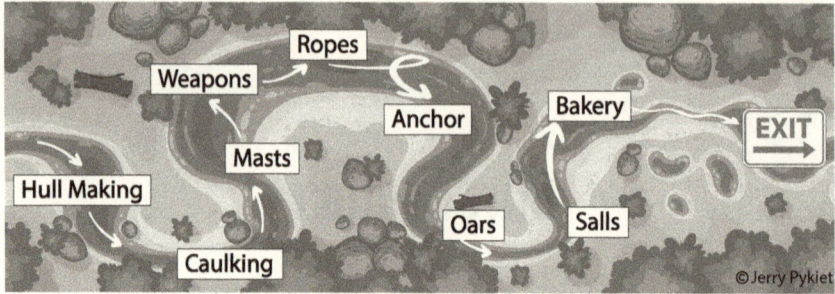

Pricing has changed in our digital age. The old way of setting prices was straightforward: cost plus profit margin equals price. This method worked well for a wealthy supplier I used to work for in the oil field business. He'd buy valves and various oil equipment at low prices and mark them up significantly because he had little competition.

For example, he'd purchase a valve for $40 and sell it for $400. The big oil companies would buy it without a second thought. This method was effective for him, but those days are long gone.

Today, the internet allows people to Google any product and compare prices instantly. The pricing game has changed. Now, the price is fixed, so the profit margin equals the price minus the cost. To stay competitive, we need to reduce costs—not by cutting employees, but by cutting waste. Reducing waste and variation helps us produce more with the same team, making our team members more valuable. It's cost-effective to pay them more and offer better benefits, ensuring they stay because now, we're really relying on these critical team members.

The shift from the old to the new pricing model requires a change in mindset. Instead of focusing on how much we can mark up a product, we need to think about how efficiently we can produce it. This means identifying and eliminating waste and variation at every step of the process. Waste can come in many forms—excess materials, unnecessary steps, or inefficient workflows.

For example, in my past experiences, we found that reorganizing the workspace to minimize the distance employees had to walk significantly boosted productivity. Small, simple changes like this can make a big difference in reducing costs and improving efficiency.

One of the most crucial aspects of this new approach is investing in our team members. When we reduce waste and variation in the processes and improve efficiency, our employees become more valuable. It's essential to pay them well and provide good benefits to keep them motivated and committed. Happy, well-compensated employees are more likely to stay with the company, reducing turnover and maintaining a high level of expertise within the team. This is a growth strategy.

The journey to efficiency doesn't stop with a single improvement. It's an ongoing process of identifying, analyzing, and eliminating waste and variation. Encouraging a culture of continuous improvement helps keep the team engaged and always looking for better ways to do things. Regularly reviewing processes and seeking input from team members can lead to innovative solutions, engaged workforce, and sustained success.

Technology plays a significant role in reducing costs and improving efficiency. Investing in the right tools and systems can streamline operations and provide valuable data for making informed decisions. From advanced manufacturing equipment to software that tracks inventory, workflow, and improvement strategies, technology can be a game-changer in staying competitive under the new pricing model.

The transition from the old way of setting prices to the new model based on reducing costs rather than inflating prices is not just about changing numbers. It is about changing the entire methodology to business. By focusing on good organization, participating with team members, incrementally continuously improving (ICI), and embracing innovation, we can thrive in this new era of pricing. The lessons from Galileo's time still hold true: innovation and productivity are key to success.

When I first heard about Incremental Continuous Improvement (ICI), I was intrigued. ICI is a methodology that promises to revolutionize the way we tackle challenges, analyze information, make conclusions, develop results, implement strategies, set objectives, and create alliances. The results? Business expansion success, complete customer satisfaction, constant waste, and process variation elimination will bring faster cycle times. It's a game-changer.

Implementing breakthrough technologies begins with developing leaders within the ICI way of thinking. This program offers a common set of tools and techniques, fostering a shared tribal language within your team. Through ICI, you'll cultivate a world-class culture—one where people feel so valued and connected that they never want to leave. Improved communication and collaboration will keep you competitive and create career opportunities for all. Ultimately, this will lead you to a dominant market position.

So, what exactly is ICI? I like to think of it as "Incremental Continuous Improvement" or, **I C**ontinuously **I**mprove by 1% every day at work. It's all about enhancing process velocity and flow while reducing difficulty. One of my favorite quotes by Leonardo da Vinci sums it up perfectly: "Simplicity is the ultimate sophistication." ICI is about continuously reducing inventories and scheduled work in progress (SWIP). Imagine a big pile of work-in-progress (WIP) between processes A and B.

At Toyota, they managed to reduce WIP by 90% in some areas, which significantly boosted process speed and flow.

Small improvements can add up to significant gains in a relatively small amount of time. Setting a goal of becoming one percent better every day can have a significant impact on yourself and your processes in just one year. Here are the numbers. If you get 1% better every day at the end of the year, you will be 37 times better. If you get 1% worse, you almost go down to zero. If you want to set a more achievable goal, you could try to get 1% better 5 days a week all year. You would still accomplish a remarkable outcome of 10 times better at the end of the year.

This is not done by setting big goals. It is done by trying to implement small Incremental Continuous Improvements (ICIs) and making that a new and powerful practice. This systematizing approach to incrementally achieving your goals will change your career trajectory and give you many wins along the way, professionally and personally.

The essence of ICI is continuously removing waste and variation from the customer's perspective. If the customer doesn't care about it or doesn't want to pay for it, it's waste. This mindset shifts the focus to what's truly valuable. For instance, when I first started implementing ICI, I realized how much unnecessary administration work we were doing. It wasn't adding value, so we reduced it, saving time and resources. Time that was better spent doing things the customer was interested in, like finding ways not to increase the cost of our products or services.

Implementing ICI is like peeling an onion—you remove one layer of waste only to find another beneath it. It is not as big of a layer, but it is still a waste. With each layer removed, processes become smoother and more efficient. This constant improvement isn't about making huge changes overnight; it's about making small, manageable tweaks that add up over time to incredible results.

One of ICI's key aspects is its emphasis on leadership development. Leaders who embrace the ICI mindset not only improve their processes but also inspire their teams to adopt the same mindset. This creates a ripple effect throughout the organization, leading to a culture of continuous improvement. In my experience, this culture is invaluable. It keeps everyone on their toes, always looking for ways to do things 1% better.

Another critical element of leveraging an ICI mindset is your reliance on data-driven decision-making. By analyzing data, you can identify bottlenecks and areas for improvement that might not be obvious at first glance. Pareto charts are beneficial when

Example of a Pareto Chart

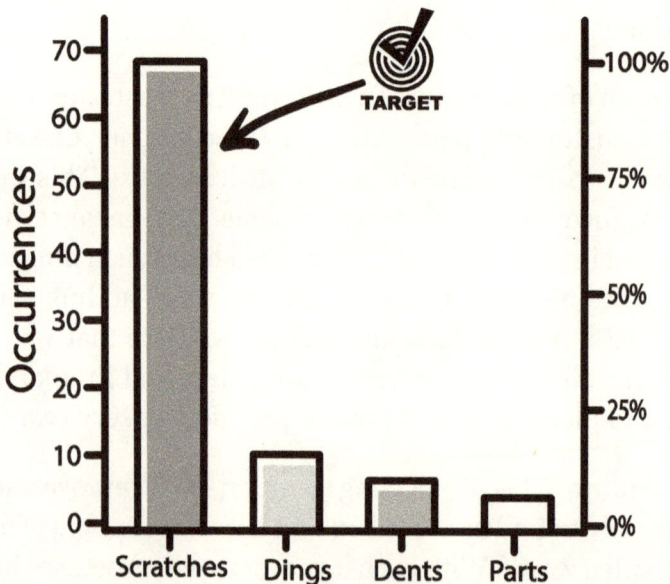

© Jerry Pykiet

you have many problems, causes, or conditions and want to find the vital few out of the trivial many. These graphs identify the 20% of categories that are responsible for 80% of the outcomes. A Pareto chart is a type of bar graph that visually represents data in descending order, where the tallest bars on the left represent the most significant factors when we started using data to drive our decisions, the results were astonishing. We could pinpoint exactly where we were wasting time and resources and address those issues directly.

ICI also emphasizes the importance of setting clear, achievable goals. Without goals, it's easy to lose direction. But with ICI, we learn to set specific, measurable objectives that keep us focused and motivated. SMART goals are a method for setting objectives that are clear, achievable, and trackable. The acronym SMART stands for:

Specific: "What do you want to accomplish, and who needs to be involved?"

Measurable: "How can you measure progress and know if you've met your goal?"

Achievable: "Do you have the skills to achieve the goal, or can you get them?"

Relevant: "Why are you setting this goal now, and is it aligned with your overall objectives?"

Time-bound: "What's the deadline, and is it realistic?"

George T. Doran first described SMART goals in print in 1981, and Professor Robert S. Ruben later expanded on the concept. This approach improved our processes and boosted morale. Everyone knew what they were working towards and could see the progress we were making.

ICI encourages a collaborative approach to developing solutions. It's not just about top-down directives; it's about involving everyone in the process. When we started involving our team members closest to the process in problem-solving, we discovered insights and solutions we would never have thought of otherwise. Their firsthand experience was invaluable, and their engagement in the process improved dramatically.

One of the most satisfying aspects of ICI is seeing tangible results. As we implemented this philosophy, we saw our cycle times decrease, our defects drop, and our customer satisfaction soar. It wasn't always easy—there were plenty of challenges along the way—but the payoff was worth it.

ICI is a powerful way of thinking that can transform your organization. By focusing on ICIs or 1% better every day, you can enhance process speed and flow, reduce complexity, and eliminate waste and process variation. Developing leaders within the ICI framework, relying on data-driven decision-making, setting clear SMART goals, and fostering a collaborative approach are all central components of this transformative approach. The result is a world-class culture, improved communication and teamwork, and ultimately, total market domination.

Sigma Levels and DMAIC

So, what does Six Sigma really mean? When we aim for 99% quality, which is about a 3.8 sigma level, we're still left with a lot of problems. To illustrate, that level of quality would mean:

- One hour of unsafe drinking water each month.
- 16,000 lost articles of US mail every hour.
- 22,000 checks deducted from the wrong bank accounts per hour.

- 500 wrong surgical operations each week.
- Two unsafe plane landings at Chicago O'Hare Airport every day.
- 50 newborn babies dropped by doctors each day.

Clearly, 99% isn't good enough in many cases. It is too much variation.

The number of defects per million varies significantly across different sigma levels. A Six Sigma level means just 3.4 defects per million products. In contrast, a five sigma company has 233 defects per million. Most companies in the US operate at three to four sigma levels.

As an example, a four sigma company has 6,210 defects per million, while a three sigma company has 66,807 defects per million. If a company operates at two sigma, it experiences 308,537 defects per million, and at one sigma, it faces a staggering

6 Sigma Principles Explained - Statistical Distribution Illustration

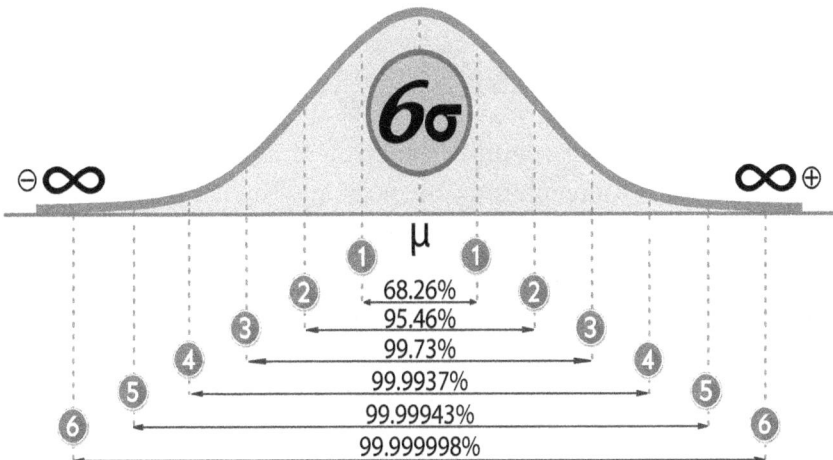

Created by Jerry Pykiet

690,000 defects per million. At these lower levels, a company is basically out of business.

The bell curve helps illustrate this concept: as you move from one sigma to six sigma, the number of defects drops dramatically. This means you're meeting customer expectations much more consistently.

The DMAIC Method

The DMAIC method, used by lawyers, doctors, and many other professionals, is a scientific approach to problem-solving. It stands for **D**efine, **M**easure, **A**nalyze, **I**mprove, and **C**ontrol. Each step helps organize your thoughts and actions, making you sound smart in meetings and ensuring you're tackling issues successfully.

Define

First, you need to identify and define the project scope with your team. Tools like a project charter are super helpful here. Clearly outline what's included in the project and what's not. Sometimes, it even helps to physically mark the scope area with caution tape for clarity. This way, everyone knows exactly what we're focusing on and where the boundaries lie.

Project charters will include the project name (Cool Name), project leader, project champion (person who owns the project), and project mentor. It is a good idea to declare one champion of the project. This person would be the one closest to the process, and everything would be approved by this person. If you go into someone's area and they start feeling out of control, you could potentially have a negative unintended consequence.

Project charters will also include problem statements, project objectives, what the project includes and does not include, customers and suppliers of the area, primary and secondary metrics (usually speed and quality), estimated savings, and an estimated phase of completion goals using DMAIC. It is important to include all the team members and have the finance representative and the top leader sign off on the project charter.

When defining your project, it's crucial to involve all stakeholders. This ensures everyone has a clear understanding of the project's goals and scope. Use visual aids like flowcharts or diagrams to illustrate the project's boundaries and objectives. For instance, if we're improving a manufacturing process, outline which stages of production are included and which are not.

Measure

Next, it's all about gathering data. Start by observing the process closely, taking before pictures, and documenting everything meticulously. To get real insights, you should go to the "Gemba," which means the actual place where the work or value is created. This hands-on approach ensures you're not just relying on secondhand information but understanding the process firsthand.

In the measuring phase, data collection accuracy is paramount. Use a variety of data collection methods, such as surveys, time studies, video recording, and sampling. Training your team in proper data collection techniques to ensure consistency is also beneficial. For example, if we're analyzing customer service response times, gather data from different time periods and customer interactions to get a comprehensive view.

Analyze

Once you've gathered your data, it's time to dive into the analysis. Determine the key performance variables by examining the data thoroughly. A good rule of thumb is to spend 90% of your time researching and just 10% solving the problem. As Einstein famously said, "If I had 10 minutes to solve a problem, I'd spend 9 minutes studying it and 1 minute solving it." Tools like fishbone diagrams, control charts, spaghetti maps, and process maps can be incredibly useful during this stage.

During the analysis stage, it's essential to look for patterns and trends in the data. Use statistical software to help identify correlations and causations. Additionally, engage with team members who are directly involved in the process—they often provide valuable insights that data alone might not reveal. For instance, if we're reducing defects in a product, involve the production staff to understand common issues and their potential causes.

CORRELATION DOES NOT IMPLY CAUSATION

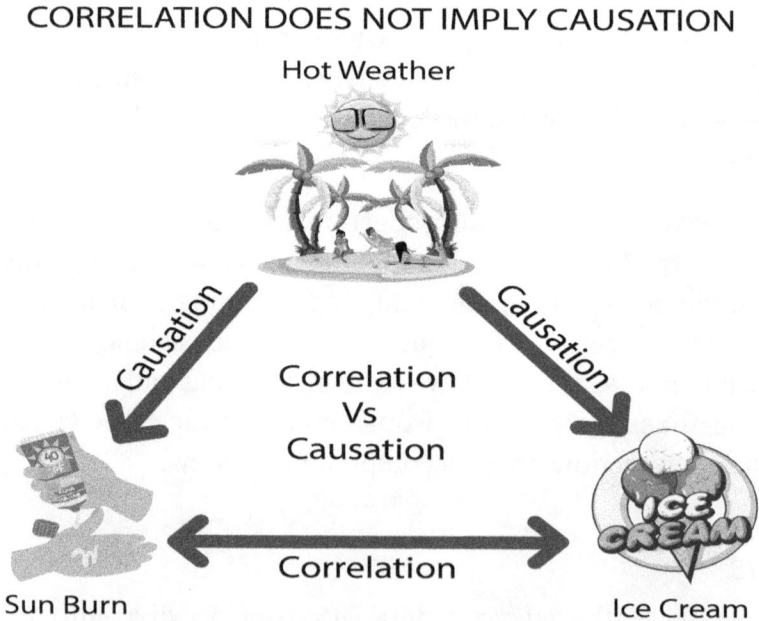

Hot Weather

Causation

Causation

Correlation
Vs
Causation

Correlation

Sun Burn

Ice Cream

© Jerry Pyklet

Improve

After analyzing the data, you need to take action based on your findings. Schedule and prioritize these actions effectively. If it's a major project, treat it with the same importance as a fishing trip or a workout session—schedule it and stick to it. By doing so, you ensure that improvements are implemented systematically and without unnecessary delays.

When it comes to making improvements, pilot testing is a great strategy. Implement changes on a small scale first to evaluate their effectiveness before a full rollout. This allows for adjustments without significant disruptions. For example, if we change a software system, test it with a small user group first to iron out any issues.

Control

Finally, you need to validate and implement a control plan to sustain the improvements you've made. Use control boards, before and after pictures, and checklists to maintain the gains. Toyota has a great philosophy: "We get brilliant results from average people managing a brilliant process. Others get average results from brilliant people managing broken processes." This highlights the importance of having robust processes in place.

Sustaining improvements requires regular monitoring and adjustments. Set up a schedule for periodic reviews of the process and outcomes. Use tools like dashboards to provide real-time updates on key performance indicators. For example, if we've implemented a new customer feedback system, regularly review the feedback to ensure the system continues to meet our goals. Some good key performance indicators (KPIs) are Safety, ICI, Quality, Delivery, Inventory, and Productivity (SIQDIP©). I remember this by thinking this dip is so sick!

Mastering the DMAIC method involves a disciplined approach to problem-solving that can transform your projects and processes. You can achieve remarkable results by defining clear scopes, measuring accurately, analyzing thoroughly, improving systematically, and controlling effectively. Remember, it's not just about making changes but about embedding continuous improvement into your company culture. This ensures sustained success and a competitive edge in your field.

3.3: Key DMAIC Questions

When using the DMAIC process, it is essential to ask the right questions at each stage. This structured approach helps identify problems, develop solutions, and ensure lasting improvements.

Let's break it down step by step:

Define

In the Define phase, you need to pinpoint which processes require improvement, so getting customer feedback is invaluable. You will need to get the voice of the customer (VOC). Clearly outline the project's objectives and scope and identify the high-level inputs and outputs.

These questions help to set a clear direction for your project:

"Which processes need improvement?"

"What customer feedback supports this?"

"What's the project's objective and scope?"

"What are the high-level inputs and outputs?"

Measure

Moving on to the Measure phase, you need to understand how the process currently operates and identify key performance measures that ensure the reliability of your measurements. This phase involves gathering accurate data to inform your analysis.

Questions to ask:

"How is the process performed?"

"What are the key performance measures?"

"How trustworthy is your measuring system?"

Analyze

In the Analyze phase, you dive into understanding the sources of variability in your process. Determine which variables you can control and identify key variables that affect performance. Spending time on analysis helps you understand the root causes of issues and prepares you for effective improvements.

Questions to ask:

"What are the sources of variability?"

"Which can you control?"

"What key variables affect performance?"

Improve

The Improve phase is all about optimizing your process and communication is key. Before full-scale implementation, it's wise to conduct a pilot test. This phase turns your analysis into actionable improvements.

Questions to ask:

> "What settings for inputs will optimize outputs?"
>
> "How will you communicate changes to stakeholders?"
>
> "Didyouconductapilotimprovementimplementation?"

Control

Finally, in the Control phase, focus on maintaining the gains you've achieved. Plan for full-scale implementation and assign ownership of the process. Reflect on your experience to apply lessons learned elsewhere. This phase ensures that improvements are sustainable and benefits are long-lasting.

Questions to ask:

> "How will you maintain gains?"
>
> "What's the plan for full-scale implementation?"
>
> "Who will own the process post-project?"
>
> "What have you learned that can be applied elsewhere?"

The DMAIC process is a powerful framework for driving continuous improvement. By asking the right questions at each stage, you can identify problems, develop effective solutions, and ensure lasting improvements. Whether you're working on a small project or a large-scale initiative, DMAIC provides a structured approach that leads to measurable results. By involving stakeholders, gathering accurate data, conducting thorough analysis, implementing targeted improvements, and maintaining control, you can achieve substantial and sustainable gains.

How Do We Learn?

Let's dive into learning techniques and how they affect retention. Did you know presentations only help us retain about 5% of what we hear? It's true. That's why, when I'm talking to my wife, I often joke that I'll only remember 5% of our conversation! It's a fun reminder of how little we actually retain just by listening.

Reading a book is a bit better; it helps us retain about 10%. Audiobooks are even more effective, boosting retention to around 20%. That is double the retention of reading. When we see demonstrations, our retention jumps to 30%. But, when we engage in discussion groups, that number goes up to 50%. This is why talking with your team is so crucial when implementing Incremental Continuous Improvement (ICI).

Now, practicing with feedback pushes retention up to 75%. This hands-on approach, combined with constructive feedback, really helps cement the knowledge. But here's the ultimate technique—teaching others. When you teach, you retain a whopping 80% of the information. It's the hardest part but also the most rewarding.

So, how can you use this information to improve your learning and teaching strategies by 1% today?

Here are some practical steps:

Presentations and Conversations

While presentations are a common method for sharing information, they shouldn't be relied upon exclusively due to their low retention rate. Whenever possible, supplement presentations with other methods to enhance retention. For instance, have a follow-up discussion or Q&A session after a presentation. This engages the audience and boosts retention.

Reading and Audiobooks

Reading is a great way to absorb information, but don't just stop at reading. Discuss the material with others or join a book club to enhance retention. Audiobooks can be a convenient alternative, especially for those who are always on the go. Listening to an audiobook while commuting or exercising can turn downtime into productive learning time.

Demonstrations

Demonstrations are powerful because they combine visual and auditory learning. Whenever you learn something new, look for video demonstrations or live workshops. If you're the one teaching, use demonstrations to show rather than just tell. For example, if you're training someone on a new software tool, a live demo can be much more effective than a simple explanation. YouTube is your friend here.

Discussion Groups

Engaging in discussion groups can significantly improve retention. Discussing a topic with colleagues gives you different perspectives and can clarify doubts. This interaction helps reinforce what you've learned. Consider joining or forming a study group, whether it's for professional development or personal interests. The collaborative environment fosters deeper understanding and retention.

Practice with Feedback

Hands-on practice is crucial for mastering any skill. But practice alone isn't enough—you need feedback to improve. Seek out opportunities for practice that include feedback, whether from a mentor, a peer, or even self-assessment tools. For example, if you're learning a new language, practice speaking with a native speaker who can correct your mistakes and offer tips for improvement.

Teaching Others

Teaching is the ultimate test of your understanding. When you teach, you have to organize your thoughts and explain concepts clearly, which deepens your own understanding. Look for opportunities to teach, whether it's formal training sessions, mentoring, or even writing articles or blog posts. Teaching can be challenging, but the rewards are immense. Not only do you solidify your own knowledge, but you also help others learn. Building people up is the best way to build yourself up by 1% daily.

Applying These Techniques in ICI

When implementing Incremental Continuous Improvement (ICI), these learning techniques become even more valuable.

Here's how you can apply them:

- **Presentations**: Use them to introduce new concepts but follow up with discussions and hands-on practice. People who present are automatically perceived as the leader.

- **Reading and Audiobooks**: Provide reading materials and audiobooks on ICI principles and case studies. Encourage team members to discuss their takeaways.

- **Demonstrations**: Show real-life examples of ICI in action. Use video demonstrations or live workshops to illustrate key points. Find fun games to build teamwork skills.

- **Discussion Groups**: Form small groups to discuss ICI strategies and share experiences. Set up recurring meetings to go where the work is done with key team members. These groups can troubleshoot problems and brainstorm ideas together.

- **Practice with Feedback**: Implement ICI strategies in small pilot projects. Provide feedback to team members on their implementation and results.

- **Teaching Others**: Encourage team members to teach what they've learned to others. This could be through formal training sessions, mentoring, or creating instructional materials. Challenge your team to strive for 1% better today.

By understanding and implementing these learning techniques, you'll see significant improvements in your processes. Better learning leads to better efficiency, higher quality, and increased satisfaction among your team and customers. It's all about creating an environment where continuous learning and improvement are part of the culture.

Mastering these learning techniques can transform the way you and your team absorb and apply new information. Whether it's through presentations, reading, discussions, practice, or teaching, each method plays a crucial role in enhancing retention and understanding. By incorporating these strategies into your daily routine, you'll not only improve your own skills but also foster a culture of ICI within your organization. So, go out, learn by doing, and then teach others. You'll be amazed at how much more you can retain and achieve.

CHAPTER 1

The 6S Program

Let me tell you about Larry Mocha. Larry built a wildly successful company that started in his garage and grew to dominate its market globally. He wanted his company to adopt a 6S (**S**afety, **S**ort, **S**et, **S**hine, **S**tandardize, **S**ustain) Lean methodology. However, three different consultants had tried and failed to implement it. Larry told me that he'd give up on this journey if I couldn't pull it off. No pressure, right? But I was determined to succeed.

When I started, I gathered all the frontline leaders in the conference room. They had been through so many failed attempts at 6S that they were skeptical and gave me dirty looks. My hands got clammy, and my back started sweating. I needed to understand their frustrations, so I asked them to share their experiences with past implementations. This was gold for me because understanding their current condition was crucial.

They started opening up about what didn't work and why. This feedback was invaluable because it showed I was listening and valued their input. I then asked them to create a wish list of everything they wanted for the project. They filled a board with requests for drills, toolboxes, and more. I took this list to Larry and told him we needed to fulfill it to show our commitment. He agreed, and we filled a quarter of the classroom with these items, proving we were serious.

One team member, who worked in the CNC cell and loved Harleys, was particularly resistant. I learned about his hobby and suggested we color-code his area with Harley colors and add Harley-themed decor. He was all in after that. By the end of the project, he told me, "Jerry, you turned my Pinto into a Cadillac," and gave me a big hug.

We repeated this process 27 times across different workstations, covering 100% of the company with a 6S program. A significant part of our success was our sustainment plan. We set up an audit program where leaders audited each area monthly with a 6S audit checklist. If a leader's area met the 6S standards, they received rewards during a monthly lunch in the large break room. This built a strong 6S culture and a world-class LEAN environment.

Understanding the 6S Program

The 6S program is a LEAN methodology designed to create a safe, organized, and efficient workplace. Here's a breakdown of each component:

1. **Safety**: Ensuring a safe working environment to prevent accidents and injuries. Build safety into your monthly 6S audits.

2. **Sort**: Removing and organizing items to reduce clutter and improve efficiency. Take "before" pics! Make kits with all your tools in them for each topic (beachfront kit, measuring kit, grinder kit, etc.). Move things out that don't belong to your Red Tag Zone.

3. **Set in Order**: Organizing necessary items so they are easy to find and use. Set items in order based on the value and make a property value map.

4. **Shine**: Set your new standard of clean like never before. Build a cleaning kit with everything you need to clean your city property. Create a 6S checklist.

5. **Standardize**: Create high-quality homes for everything (parking spaces, bins, shadow boards, etc.). Visually control the flow of information with labels, lines, color codes, Kanbans, poka-yokes, SOPs, large signs, etc.

6. **Sustain**: Establish standards and procedures to maintain the first three S's. Continuously following and improving upon these practices to ensure long-term success.

When I took on Larry's projects, I knew I had to address the skepticism and resistance from the frontline leaders. Their past experiences with failed 6S implementations had left them disheartened. To gain their trust, I made it clear that their input was crucial. Listening to their stories and frustrations allowed me to understand the root causes of previous failures and allowed them to blow off some steam.

One major issue was the lack of proper tools and equipment. By creating a wish list and fulfilling it, we showed the team that we were committed to providing the resources they needed. This small but significant gesture helped build trust and demonstrated our seriousness about the 6S program.

Personalization was key to winning over resistant team members. For instance, the CNC cell worker who loved Harleys was initially very resistant to the 6S changes. By incorporating his passion for Harleys into the workspace design, we made the process more appealing to him. This approach transformed his attitude from resistance to enthusiastic participation. The CNC operator's feedback, "Jerry, you turned my Pinto into a Cadillac," was a testament to the effectiveness of personalizing the implementation. This incentivized adherence to the 6S principles and fostered a sense of community and recognition.

Implementing the 6S program across 27 workstations was significant, but sustaining it was equally important. We developed an audit program where leaders would audit each area monthly using a 6S checklist. This regular review process ensured that the standards were maintained.

The combination of consistent audits, rewards, and a strong emphasis on safety, organization, and cleanliness helped us build a world-class LEAN environment. The success of our 6S program was evident in the improved efficiency (over 2x in some areas), reduced waste, and enhanced workplace morale. A positive workplace morale helps safety and employee turnover and increases the output of the entire organization.

The journey to implement the 6S program was challenging but incredibly rewarding. We transformed the company's work environment by listening to the frontline leaders, fulfilling their needs, personalizing the approach, and establishing a robust sustainment plan. The 6S program not only improved operational efficiency but also created a safer and more enjoyable workplace. This experience taught me the power of commitment, personalization, and continuous incremental improvement in achieving lasting success.

1S Safety

Safety is always the top priority in my 6S program. That is why I moved it to the top of 6S. Most implementers have it at the bottom, which always seemed strange. The 6S flow is **S**afety, **S**ort, **S**et, **S**hine, **S**tandardize, **S**ustain. A good practice is to have people from outside the area conduct safety audits before, during, and after each project. Fresh eyes can spot issues that those familiar with the area might overlook. Including safety in your 6S audit program ensures that a team is always looking for and addressing safety issues.

Expanding on 6S for Safety

Safety is more than just a word—it's a commitment; it is how your neurons flow in your brain. When we talk about the 6S methodology, safety always comes first. This isn't just a procedural step; it's a culture. Implementing safety in every phase of 6S ensures that it becomes second nature to everyone involved.

Daily production meetings should kick off with a safety discussion. Make it the first topic of conversation. This sets the tone for the day and keeps safety at the forefront of everyone's mind. The first thing the leader talks about is the most important topic. It's not just about compliance; it's about creating an environment where everyone feels responsible for each other's well-being.

2S Sort

In the Sort phase, always take before pictures from consistent positions, usually from each corner or the middle. Some use paint or stickers in the shape of feet to mark where to stand for these pictures. This helps you see progress clearly. Sorting involves organizing inventory into kits, much like packing when you move out of your home. We normally label boxes with contents like "kitchen" or "PlayStation stuff" instead of randomly throwing items together. If you don't organize as you are clearing everything out, you could lose friends when you start to put it back together.

Eliminate unneeded items by red-tagging them. Red tagging means placing unneeded items in a designated area without worrying about ownership. This speeds up the decision-making process. The leader owns the red tag zone and decides what to do with the items within one or two weeks. For long-term red tag storage, wrap and label items, then place them in low-value areas (like a top shelf in the north 40). It is key to create a clean canvas by removing all unnecessary items and clutter to create your masterpiece. This helps you see the potential of the area and reimagine its setup.

Diving Deeper into the Sort Phase

The Sort phase of 6S is all about organization. This way, you know exactly what's inside each box and can find things easily when you need them.

Next, sort through everything and organize inventory into kits. This step is crucial for efficiency. When everything is organized and labeled, you can find tools and materials quickly, reducing downtime and frustration. Then, you will see that you could have seven or eight of the same things or find some things that need replacing or upgrading. Everything in the scope of the 6S project will be cleaned, fixed, painted, or replaced.

Now, let's talk a little more about red tagging. Some folks paint a big red table in the middle of the shop for a permanent red tag zone. That way, anyone can eliminate things they don't want or need and keep the shop or office clutter-free. Usually, the temporary 6S project red tag is just a box with red tag written on it or a pallet with boxes on it that say red tag.

It is important to have a red tag zone before starting your project. The red tag zone will help relieve anxiety for the area owners. Most of the time, they have an emotional attachment to their items. I like to tell them that we are not going to throw away anything that isn't obvious trash. It is best to have the area owner be the champion of the project, and the rest of the team supports the champion while they are busy making decisions.

During the Sort phase, ask yourself and your team a series of questions to ensure thoroughness: Are there broken, unused, or unneeded items? Are personal items properly stored? Is there any clutter? Are trash cans being used? Is there hidden junk?

Later, ask yourself, are red-tagged items older than three weeks?

3S Set

Setting everything in order in your workspace is crucial for good organization and keeping your sanity. Think of your workspace like real estate: beachfront property, city property, deserted island, and outer space.

Beachfront property is where the value is created, like a welder's station, where tools must be within three feet or three seconds of the welder's blue light. The blue light is what you see when the welder is welding. Welders are easy to see when waste is being created. When that blue light turns off the waste has begun. Some of the waste is of no value but cannot be avoided. If the welder must move around to weld in different locations, I like to build them a custom cart and tell them we will build you a custom camper (cart), just like your camper at home. It has everything you need in it for your week-long adventure.

City property represents your immediate workspace. This is your office or work cell. I like to call it your home or your casa. You can make this fun by naming it like The I.T. Penthouse, Paradise Island, Fast and Furious, or Hotel California. This allows people to put up some small décor to theme their area. In a time of high turnover and low morale, this can be a competitive advantage because you are allowing them to do something no other employer would let them do. Thus, reducing turnover and increasing profits. I gave an assembly line a tropical theme once with exotic fake birds and palm trees. The owner thought I was crazy until the production doubled, and then he came up to me and said, "More palm trees, Jerry, this is working."

The deserted island zone is for items you use infrequently. These are stored further away from your main workspace, indicating something is wrong. If you find yourself accessing this area often, this will indicate a defect in your layout. These could be seasonal tools or backup supplies. Keeping them here prevents clutter in the more critical zones and ensures they're still available when needed.

Outer space is for items you rarely use or must go to the store to pick up. Accessing this zone should be avoided unless absolutely necessary because it takes significant time and effort. These items should only be needed once in a blue moon. It is nice to have these terms in your tribal language. It is better to ask someone, "Why are you in outer space? I am just concerned for your safety out here?" than, "What the heck are you doing on the other side of the facility all the time?".

Expanding on Setting in order

Setting in order involves more than just placing items where they seem to fit; it's about creating a logical, efficient layout that minimizes wasted time and effort.

Let's break down each "real estate" zone for clarity:

Beachfront Property

Beachfront property is the prime real estate of your workspace. This is where the most critical tasks occur, where value is created for your customers, and items in this zone should be easily accessible. Your most frequently used tools should be within arm's reach (3 ft—3 sec.). Anything you use multiple times daily should be in this immediate area to save time and reduce movement.

Imagine you just inherited 1,000 feet of beachfront property in Hawaii with nothing on it. You would like to find a way to generate an income from this property. You probably wouldn't build one big palace and move in. That would be an over-production waste. You would probably leverage the property for a loan and build the tallest tower you can with small condos in them that fit 2 to 4 people for a short burst of time. Then you could charge top dollar for very small bins of property and refill the bins every 3 to 7 days with paying customers. Then, with the millions you would be making, you could go and buy a nice beachfront property already constructed just the way you like and live like a rock star.

While watching Cribs (a TV show about rock stars' lifestyles) one day, I noticed that these rock stars never leave their palaces. Why would they? Everything they need is in their homes. They have bowling, indoor swimming, hair salons, doctors making house calls, gyms, arcade rooms, home theaters, and much more. I would never want to leave their fantasy land. This concept is no different than building your own beachfront property at work or at home.

When building an assembly cell, welding cart (custom camper), office cubical, or front desk for a business, you want everything they would need in their beachfront property so they would never have to leave. You would set it up just like you did the condos you now own in Hawaii. You would have small bins that would only hold what you need for the next 3 to 7 days. Then, set up Kanban systems (visual refill indicators) for all your consumables. This way, you don't take up too much space and still have everything you need 3 feet or 3 seconds away from where you create value for your customer. We will talk more about Kanban systems later in the book.

©Jerry Pykiet

City Property

Think of city property as the area just beyond your immediate reach but still within easy access. It's like having a convenience store beside your house rather than driving across town. Tools and materials in this zone should be organized so you can quickly find and use them without leaving your workstation.

This is your office, cubicle, work cell, or your garage. You don't travel far for daily items, just like you wouldn't drive to another city for milk. If I told my wife that I was leaving our small town in the country to go to Tulsa for milk, she would immediately call out a defect and probably start a root cause analysis by asking why five times. I completely adore my beautiful wife, so I would never go to Tulsa for milk. That being said. You should ask yourself during the set process. "What is my milk in my workstation?" and "Am I walking to Tulsa daily to get it?".

Deserted Island

Your deserted island is outside your immediate area. This would be like walking to the other side of the office or shop to ask questions or get resources. This would indicate something's wrong if you must go there often. You want to decide to go and talk with your friends or coworkers. By having the inventory on a deserted island, the inventory is controlling you and making you get up and walk around. I love walking around and collaborating with people, but I want to make that decision for myself, not the inventory telling me what to do and when. Take control of your inventory so it does not control you.

Outer Space

Outer space is like going to Office Depot or Home Depot—high-risk and time-consuming. If you go to outer space, you will have to suit up and tether up. This is risky, and we don't know if you're even going to make it back. You should avoid it unless absolutely necessary.

To successfully implement the Set in Order phase, follow these steps:

1. **Mapping Zones**: Use a whiteboard or digital tool to map out your workspace. Clearly define the beachfront, city, deserted island zones, and outer space. Mark these areas physically in your workspace using tape, signs, or paint to ensure everyone knows where each zone starts and ends. You could own multiple beachfronts.

2. **Organizing Cabinets**: For cabinets, consider the ergonomic height for frequently used items. Store these at a comfortable reach (beachfront property). Items used less frequently can go on shelves just above and below this (city property). Reserve the highest and lowest shelves (deserted island) for the least used items, or don't use them at all and remove the shelf so it doesn't become cluttered.

3. **Labeling**: Clearly label all storage areas and containers. Use color coding or signboards to make it easy to find and return items. For example, tools could have color-coded tags that match labels on the storage bins.

4. **Visual Management**: Implement visual management tools like shadow boards for tools, which outline where each tool belongs. This makes it easy to find tools and to see immediately if something is missing.

4S Shine

The Shine phase is about more than just cleanliness; it's about creating a workspace that enhances productivity and safety. Set your new standard of cleanliness like never before. If you can see it, it must be cleaned. Build a cleaning kit with everything you need to clean your city property. Create a 6S Checklist.

Here are some practical tips:

1. **Daily Cleaning Routine**: Establish a daily cleaning routine. Assign specific tasks to team members and make it a part of their daily schedule. This routine should include wiping down surfaces, organizing tools, and emptying trash cans.

2. **Cleaning Kits**: Each work area should have a dedicated cleaning kit. This avoids the hassle of searching for cleaning supplies and encourages regular cleaning. Stock the kit with essential items like cleaning sprays, cloths, and dustpans. Ideally the cleaning kit is on a shadow board or a visually controlled cart.

3. **Inspection and Maintenance**: Regularly inspect the workspace for wear and tear with a 6S Checklist to ensure you are not missing anything. Everything will be cleaned, fixed, painted, or replaced within your city property. This not only keeps the area looking good but also ensures the equipment is in good working condition by allowing you to spot problems quickly, like leaks or wear and tear, that might otherwise go unnoticed.

4. **Root Cause Analysis**: When something isn't maintained, don't just clean it up. Understand why it happened. If you have one problem, you have two problems. You have the original problem, and you have the root cause of the original problem that needs to be solved. Conduct a root cause analysis by asking "why" five times. This helps identify underlying issues and prevents them from recurring.

Implementing the Safety, Sort, Set and Shine phases of the 6S program can transform your workspace into an efficient, safe, and productive environment that is enjoyable to be in. By thoughtfully organizing your tools and materials and maintaining a clean workspace, you set the stage for continuous improvement and operational excellence. Remember, the key to success lies in being dedicated, diligent, and data-driven to these principles. Regular 6S audits, clear communication systems, and a culture of continuous improvement will ensure that the benefits of the 6S program are sustained long-term.

5S Standardize

Standardizing involves creating procedures and schedules to maintain the new order. This could include daily cleaning 6S checklists, weekly or monthly 6S audits, and regular 6S training sessions to ensure everyone understands their roles and responsibilities. Consistency is key here.

Standardizing processes and organizing tools isn't just about simplicity. It's about effectiveness and consistency. If something can be moved, it needs a designated home so you can tell at the end of the day that it is missing. Tools and consumables can travel around during the day but like me, I need a home to go to so my family would know I was missing. Imagine a chaotic parking lot full of snow in the winter where you can't find your car. That's what a disorganized workspace feels like. By assigning specific "parking spots" for tools and equipment, you can always find what you need quickly.

Practical Steps to Standardization

1. **Outline Shapes and Color-Code Areas**: Use tape, paint or 6S foam to outline the shapes of tools on workbenches or pegboards. If a tool can move, it needs to be outlined on the walls and the floors. This visual cue helps workers know exactly where each tool belongs. Color-coding these areas can make it even easier. Having a specific color for each city property can improve company culture. Color coding is a key communication tool so that everyone knows who owns what tool.

   For example, Tom borrows an air tool from Jerry and uses it for a couple of weeks. Now, Tom has forgotten that he borrowed the air tool and thinks it is his. Jerry gets upset and spites (Desire to hurt, annoy, or offend someone) Tom for the next couple of months. This behavior slows down productivity and damages your company culture. It also can start a tool domino effect. Say Jerry goes and takes someone else's air tool, and that person takes someone else's air tool until everyone in the shop has stolen from each other, and spite behavior becomes the new normal.

When we work together, we have a choice: spite, fight, or collaboration. Collaboration is ideal; if someone verbally wants to fight me, at least I know what is going on and can defuse the situation. Spite can be invisible, and sometimes, we can do it and not even realize it. Let's design our areas so that the only road we go down is Collaboration Lane and enjoy getting into our flow at work.

2. **Labels and Signage**: Clearly label all storage areas. This includes tool racks, shelves, and bins. Labels should be easy to read and understand, ensuring anyone can find and return tools without confusion. Some labels can have pictures or QR codes that go to what the part is and what it is used for. Labels work well when color-coded, magnetic, and of the highest quality. Labels must add value to the process.

If you start labeling a light switch, light switch, then it will become a joke, and you will lose your momentum. If you say what the light switch goes to, like the left side and right side, then you are on the right track. Signage is often overlooked. Remember, we are not doing this for the expert who has worked in the area for many years. We are doing this for the new employees so they can quickly become valuable to our team. Big, professional-looking signs that tell what department you are in or what you are building are great for plant tours and help the team keep a consistent tribal language when talking about where they are going and what they are doing.

3. **Team Preferences and Themes**: Get your team involved by letting them choose color schemes or themes. This personal touch can make the process more engaging. For instance, if a team loves the Buffalo Bills, use red and blue for their workspace. This not only helps with organization but also boosts team morale. These personal touches can help you take something that can seem boring and make it fun. Sometimes, I will get stickers of the team logo and use them for color coding. Be cautious of your theme. You want it to be easily transferable so that when people move around, it works for everyone. Themes must be approved by top leadership to avoid having an inappropriate theme.

4. **Durable Materials**: Invest in high-quality materials for outlining and labeling. ULINE or 3M tape, 6S foam boards, paint pens, metal-solvent dye, and 3D Puff Paint are durable options that can withstand daily wear and tear. The goal is to create a system that lasts so you don't have to redo it frequently. Be sure to thoroughly clean the surface before applying your visual controls. The only way you are going to be able to do a "controlled scientific experiment" is to have all our variables in control and have high-quality visual controls to help do the job.

   Imagine that you are getting ready to teach someone how to hunt. You have one student who holds the weapon sideways, breathes erratically, hunches over sometimes, wears different outfits every time, and holds the weapon inconsistently. The result of them hitting the target is all over the place. Your other student has every variable in control. They liked the show Myth Busters, so they prepared for this training by controlling all variables. The results of your second student hitting the target is a very tight spread but just a little off-center. All you must do is show them how to hold their finger properly. Which student would you want to pick to represent you in the upcoming competition?

5. **Play Books**: We must operate the same way every time until we can prove a better way with the stopwatch. Imagine going to a Cowboys football game, and the cheerleaders all have their own special way of doing kicks and jumping. They would not look like they are a team and be hard to watch. You do not see professional teams doing the same task differently. If everyone is doing the same kick or jump, it is easy to make improvements. You change one thing, and it can change everything. All the way the same way.

When you get close to the end of your project, get with your team and find the one way that everyone will do the job. This is not easy, and it doesn't have to be perfect. Once you find the one way, put it into an SOP checklist with times next to each batch of steps. This will become the new standard that we all have to follow until a better way is found and agreed on.

Creating playbooks for different demand levels is critical. A playbook is your SOP with a diagram on the right side of the page that shows the movements with a layout of the work area/station and arrows that correlate with the SOP checklist. The playbook will change when demand increases or decreases. You may have to add two people and divide the playbook into three or four team members. This process is tedious, but without a playbook and the leaders making sure the team members are following it, we will never get the results that our masterpiece is capable of.

6S Sustain

The success of the 6S program doesn't just come from initial implementation—it's about sustaining these practices long-term. It takes just as much work to sustain a 6S program as it does to build one.

Consider these questions:

> "Are floors and workstations clearly marked?"
>
> "Is there a specific place for everything?"
>
> "Are visual aids like color coding and signboards in use?"
>
> "Ask yourself, "Would you feel comfortable giving our top customer a tour of this area?" "Are you ready right now for the perfect plant tour?"
>
> "Is the 6S program discussed at key meetings?"
>
> "Are safety risks addressed quickly?"

Sustaining a 6S program is challenging because it requires ongoing effort and commitment. It's not a one-time project but a continuous process that must be integrated into the daily routine.

Key Strategies for Sustainability

1. **Management Support and Accountability**: For 6S to succeed, management must allocate time and resources for its upkeep. If 6S is important, we schedule a time to practice it. I like to track the individual team members' hard and soft savings in minutes saved for the year. Hard savings are calculated by multiple time studies and soft savings are not measured by a stopwatch but could add value in the future or make the environment safer.

To hold everyone accountable, include 6S responsibilities in yearly performance reviews and their hard and soft savings. When employees know their efforts are recognized and evaluated, they're more likely to maintain high standards.

2. **Reward and Recognition**: Celebrating achievements can significantly boost motivation. Develop a reward system tailored to what your team values most. Whether it's gift cards, extra time off, public recognition, or a traveling trophy, these incentives can keep the momentum going. I like to make custom traveling trophies that they would be proud to take pictures with and show their family. I have spent over a thousand dollars on some traveling trophies.

You can also make custom badges they can mount on their communication board to show how many times they have won. But remember, consistency is key. If you start a reward program, don't stop abruptly, as it can demotivate the team just as much as motivate if managed incorrectly. It's best if you make doing 6S part of the company culture. If you are on the right track, you will hear your team positively start saying, "6S and ICI is just what we do here".

Encourage friendly competitions between different teams or departments. For example, the team that saves the most hard minutes this month and keeps up with 6S responsibilities will get the traveling trophy, and the top leaders will take them out for lunch. Offer prizes or other incentives for the best-performing group based on measurable time saved. This not only drives improvement but also fosters a spirit of camaraderie and healthy competition.

3. **Integration into Meetings**: Discuss the 6S program in key meetings, ideally right after safety updates. I like to have a quick morning kickoff meeting to set the tone for the day and discuss your SIQDIP© (Safety, ICI, Quality, Delivery, Inventory, and Productivity). This practice of discussing your SIQDIP© at the beginning of meetings underscores its importance and keeps it at the top of mind for everyone. Regularly addressing SIQDIP© in meetings reinforces its relevance and encourages ongoing participation. If top leadership does not discuss SIQDIP© , the team will see that it is not important, and you could lose your team's improvement momentum.

4. **Quick Response to Safety Risks**: Address safety risks promptly to show your commitment to a safe work environment. Rapid responses to identified risks demonstrate that management takes safety seriously and is committed to maintaining a safe workspace. The faster you respond to Safety and ICIs, the more you will see it energize your team, and the speed of change will increase.

5. **Visual Management**:

   Visual management is everything that visually controls your process and inventory. It is key to make them as high quality as possible to show how important your 6S program is to you and the company. You are not doing 6S if you are not visually controlling everything in your work areas. Creating lines for walkways and signs for each area or department. Labeling and creating homes for everything that can move, utilizing playbooks, and color coding will separate your brand from all the rest and give you a competitive advantage that your competition will not be able to catch up to.

Use 6S display boards in each work cell to track progress. These boards should include, but not be limited to, 6S checklists, audit scores, and before-and-after pictures. Visual documentation of before-and-after pictures for your area will show how much work you put into building it, and your new team members will see it and respect you and your area more.

Think about driving by a big mansion with big columns out front and fancy cars parked around the fountain. Some people might say, "They probably inherited it. They probably didn't even work for it". Now think if you met the person with the big mansion and he pulled an old picture from his wallet of a crooked old shack that looked like it was run down and in a bad location, and he told you it was the first house he purchased when he was 26 years old.

If you saw this picture and learned that the mansion guy struggled, took big risks, and made big sacrifices his entire life to get where he is today, you would have more respect for him. That is why before and after pictures are important to display in every area. Having a good 6S display board also provides a constant reminder of the standards everyone is working to uphold.

The sustain phase is about making 6S part of the organizational culture. Recognize and reward teams that maintain high standards. This will help everyone stay motivated and also reinforce the importance of the 6S methodology. It is important that the recognition is completely customized to the team members and what they value.

Building and sustaining a 6S program requires effort, commitment, and strong leadership. By setting everything in order and maintaining cleanliness, you create a workspace that's efficient, safe, and pleasant to work in. Regular audits, ongoing training, involving the team in the process and commitment to ICI can make a significant difference to the bottom line of the business. Remember, sustaining these practices is just as challenging as implementing them. With management support, accountability, and a culture of recognition, you can maintain a high standard and drive continuous improvement across your organization. This will dramatically enhance job satisfaction and safety for everyone involved.

Implementing the 6S program can transform your work environment. By prioritizing safety, organizing efficiently, and maintaining a high standard of visual controls, you can create a workspace that is both productive and enjoyable. The journey requires dedication from the top down, but the financial and cultural rewards are well worth the effort. So, take these steps, involve your team, and watch as your workspace evolves into a model of LEAN efficiency and safety

CHAPTER 2

The Power of One Shadow Board

One shadow board can change everything. I was working with a large manufacturing company that spanned 40-50 acres and had seven different welding shops scattered across the area. They had about 150 employees, and the place felt like a chaotic gang culture. On my first tour, it was pure chaos. Two forklifts collided, and they explained that they had high turnover and went through a lot of temp workers.

I knew we needed to find the right person to lead this transformation, someone who could adapt well and champion the project. We chose a high school football referee and decided to make his work area themed like a football stadium, with black and white colors. We started by creating a world-class shadow board right in the middle of the shop. Many doubted this idea, thinking all the tools would end up in a pawn shop within a month.

We spent countless hours making this shadow board high-quality. We installed a laser-cut sign on top, labeled "Referee's Call," and used a metal pegboard with a light on top, shelves at the bottom, and a roll cage around it. We invested over $2,000 in this one large shadow board. By making this a first-class shadow board, people respected it, and not a single tool was taken. Even after a year, nothing was missing. Just changing one thing can change everything.

World-Class Culture

When I give classes or seminars, I often ask, "What is world-class culture?" The team usually looks stunned because culture is a strange word to define. To me, culture is simply the way you do things around here—how you behave. Every family has a culture at their dinner table. Some families might belch, cuss, and say crude things. In my house, we try to be polite and kind and avoid arguing. We eat with our mouths closed—that's our culture.

Families and communities have cultures for celebrating and partying. It's just the way we like to do things. When I ask about a company's culture, responses vary from "They scream at me" to "They treat me well and give rewards." A world-class culture is a place nobody wants to leave. So, what would it take to be a company that nobody wants to leave?

The concept of the shadow board was simple but powerful. It was more than just an organizational tool; it was a statement. By creating a designated spot for every tool, we introduced a sense of order and respect for the workplace. This board wasn't just about knowing where things were; it was about changing the mindset of everyone who used it.

Finding the right person to lead the transformation was critical. We chose a high school football referee because of his ability to maintain order and fairness under pressure. His work area, themed like a football stadium, symbolized the discipline and organization we aimed to instill. Creating the shadow board was a meticulous process, but the real investment was in changing the company's culture.

The skepticism we faced was intense. This small change began to shift the entire culture. People started taking pride in their workspaces. The order and respect introduced by one shadow board began to spread throughout the company.

Developing a World-Class Culture

Creating a world-class culture is about more than just policies and procedures. It's about the daily behaviors and attitudes of everyone in the organization.

Here are some steps to help build a world-class culture:

1. **Define Your Culture**

   Start by defining what your culture looks like. Just as every family has its own dinner table culture, every company has its unique way of doing things. What behaviors do you want to encourage? What values are most important?

2. **Lead by Example**

   Leadership plays a crucial role in shaping culture. Leaders must model the behaviors they want to see in their teams. If respect, kindness, and hard work are valued, leaders should exemplify these traits.

3. **Involve Everyone**

   Building a culture isn't just a top-down process. Involve everyone in the organization by seeking their input and encouraging their participation. Create opportunities for employees to contribute to the culture in meaningful ways.

4. **Recognize and Reward**

Recognition and rewards are powerful tools for rein-
forcing desired behaviors. Celebrate achievements and
acknowledge those who embody the company's values.
Custom rewards based on what team members value
most can motivate them.

5. **Maintain and Adapt**

Culture isn't static. It requires ongoing effort to maintain and adapt. Review your culture initiatives regularly
and make adjustments as needed. Stay committed to the
principles that define your organization.

The power of one shadow board in transforming a chaotic
workplace into a well-organized, respectful environment
cannot be overstated. It wasn't just about organizing
tools; it was about changing mindsets and behaviors. This
small change had a ripple effect, influencing the entire
company culture.

Similarly, building a world-class culture requires defining what that culture looks like, leading by example,
involving everyone, recognizing and rewarding desired
behaviors, and continuously maintaining and adapting
the culture. When done right, a world-class culture is a
place where no one wants to leave—a place where everyone feels valued, respected, and motivated to contribute
their best.

Culture Eats Strategy for Breakfast

Over the years, one of the most important lessons I've learned is
embodied in the statement, "Culture eats strategy for breakfast."
This simple yet profound idea has shaped my approach to

business and leadership. You see, no matter how brilliant a company's strategy might be, if the culture is toxic, it will drag down employee performance and, ultimately, the success of the entire company.

A bad culture is like a heavy anchor, pulling everything down with it. It demoralizes employees, stifles innovation, and creates an environment where even the best strategies can't thrive. But here's the silver lining: culture can be changed. It's not set in stone. The first step towards transforming a bad culture is for management to acknowledge its existence. Leaders must recognize that they have either created or allowed a negative culture to persist. This isn't always easy, but it's crucial.

Change must start from the top. Leaders must set the tone and lead by example. When management shows a commitment to change, it sends a powerful message to everyone in the organization. It's like a ripple effect – when the top levels of management embrace a positive culture, it gradually spreads throughout the company.

Improving culture is the most effective way to enhance company performance. It's not just about implementing new policies or offering perks. It's about creating an environment where employees feel valued, respected, and motivated to do their best work. When people are happy and engaged, they're more productive, more creative, and more likely to go the extra mile.

I remember a time in my own career when I witnessed a dramatic cultural shift within a company I was working for. The management team recognized that the existing culture was toxic and decided to take action. They started by openly communicating their commitment to change. They involved employees at all levels in the process, seeking their input and feedback. It wasn't an overnight transformation, but gradually, the atmosphere began to improve. People started to feel more connected and motivated, and the company's performance improved significantly.

Creating a positive culture is an ongoing effort that requires consistent attention and dedication. Leaders need to continuously assess their organization's cultural health and be willing to adjust as needed. It's about fostering open communication, encouraging collaboration, and recognizing and rewarding positive behaviors.

One practical step towards improving culture is clearly defining and communicating the company's values and mission. When employees understand and align with these core principles, they feel a greater sense of purpose and belonging. Another important aspect is providing opportunities for growth and development. When people see a path for advancement and feel supported in their professional journey, they're more likely to stay engaged and committed.

Moreover, it's essential to create a culture of trust and transparency. Leaders should be approachable and open to feedback. When employees feel that their voices are heard and their contributions matter, it fosters a sense of ownership and pride in their work.

"Culture eats strategy for breakfast" isn't just a catchy phrase – it's a powerful truth. A positive culture is the foundation upon which successful strategies are built. By recognizing the importance of culture and committing to nurturing a positive environment, leaders can drive significant improvements in performance and achieve lasting success. So, let's focus on building a culture where everyone can thrive and watch how it transforms our business.

High-Performance Companies vs. Typical Companies

Let's compare high-performance companies to typical companies using the time usage of Deming's prize-winning companies. High-performance companies spend their time on important, non-urgent issues. In contrast, typical companies spend most of their time on urgent, non-important issues.

High-performance companies focus on developing their people, creating standard operating procedures, aligning performance and KPIs with world-class standards, and working on cultural improvement programs. On the other hand, typical companies get caught up in urgent, non-important tasks, like loading trucks during important training sessions or taking unnecessary phone calls.

You need to ask yourself, what are the important, non-urgent issues in your company? These include developing people, creating SOPs, and improving culture. Urgent, non-important issues are distractions that can often wait, like loading trucks or answering non-critical phone calls. We need to rewire our brains to focus on the important tasks and schedule other issues for later.

Understanding and implementing these concepts can significantly change how your company operates. By focusing on culture and prioritizing important issues, you can create a world-class environment where employees thrive and want to stay.

CHAPTER 3

Performance Mapping

I was working at a factory in Florida on the Atlantic coast when I met Sean. He was an amazing guy who had been working there for 15 years. At that time, I had a partner, a LEAN expert with many years of experience. We approached Sean and said, "Hey, Sean, we're going to do a little mapping exercise." We introduced him to spaghetti mapping, which is like your cookie crumb trail on your GPS. It shows everywhere you walk from the beginning to the end of your process.

We asked Sean to demonstrate how he built one of the winding units for boat lifts. He picked up a 75-pound unit off the ground as if it weighed nothing and handed it to me. I jumped back, amazed at his strength. Sean had spent the last 10-15 years bending down, lifting, and walking, all because the inventory controlled him.

I told Sean, "Let's make it so you can control the inventory, not the other way around." My partner and I made quick blueprints of the shop, started drawing, and had Sean walk us through his process from start to finish. The shop had five bays, each 50 by 100 feet, and Sean hit all five. His spaghetti map was a mess of lines, making it clear he walked an incredible distance daily.

We calculated that Sean walked the equivalent of crossing the country and back multiple times each year. To solve this, we invested in high-quality carts with the company logo, custom-made to fit all the parts. This change meant Sean never had to leave his "beachfront property"—his value-added location. He went from walking miles to staying within three feet, three seconds of everything he needed.

Mind Mapping and Process Mapping

Mind mapping is a collaborative exercise where everyone throws out ideas that can build on each other. Recently, we worked on a mission statement and started with "mission statement philosophy." Everyone contributed elements like production systems, success, visual factories, and incremental continuous improvement. We ended up with a digital Visio document with "mission statement philosophy" in the middle with a big circle around it. Then, I started little circles around it with high-level thoughts and put circles connecting those thoughts with lower-level thoughts. In the end, we had a big mind map that clearly communicated what was in everyone's head. One of my favorite mission statements that came from my good friend was "Serving others, building people, and pursuing excellence."

Process mapping categorizes workflow key elements like inputs, outputs, activity steps, and decision points. It breaks down processes into simple visual steps to identify problem areas and improvement opportunities. The purpose is to gain knowledge and document work so it can be improved. Tools for process mapping include freehand drawings, Post-it notes, templates, and software like Microsoft Excel, PowerPoint, Visio, and LucidCharts.

A practical approach is to use a wall or whiteboard with Post-it notes and involve subject matter experts (SMEs). Start by asking,

"What's the first step?" Ideally, do this in the Gemba (where the work is done) or in an office or training room. I once did this with 29 engineers, and none of them knew the processes. Getting agreement on each step can be challenging, like figuring out a consistent way to brush your teeth; once some of the team members find out that some other team members leave the water on while brushing, the performance is on, and it can take hours, but it's essential.

We'll discuss various process maps, from least to most complex:

> SIPOC: Captures information critical to a project.
>
> Simple Process Flow: A checklist of activities from start to finish.
>
> Swim Lane Diagram: A process flow that switches departments.
>
> Process Observation: Observing and documenting the process.
>
> Spaghetti Diagram: Traces physical flow.
>
> Time Value Map: Shows time spent on each process step.
>
> Value Stream Map: Most complex but very powerful.

SIPOC

SIPOC stands for Suppliers, Inputs, Process, Outputs, and Customers. It's a process snapshot that verifies inputs match outputs and expectations. Here's a fun way to teach it: Imagine someone wins six million dollars and wants to throw a party. Identify the party's customers (friends, family, neighbors), the desired outputs (happy guests), the process (party planning), inputs (food, drinks, entertainment), and suppliers (stores, vendors).

Once, I taught this to 33 welders, and they loved it. One welder used the SIPOC method to help his wife plan a wedding, making him a hero at home.

Swim Lane Flowcharts

Swim lane flowcharts are great for communication issues or defects. They show the process flow across different departments, highlighting where defects occur. Each column represents a department (customer, sales, engineering, etc.), and the flowchart shows how the process moves through these departments. Whenever the process goes back upstream, it's a red flag indicating a problem.

Process Observation Chart Mapping

Observing a process in action gives a deep understanding of reality and sparks improvement ideas. Plan your observations and use video recording when applicable. Aim for at least seven observations, though 31 would be ideal for scientific accuracy. Average the observations to create a baseline for understanding the process and identifying waste and variation.

Spaghetti Process Mapping

Spaghetti mapping depicts the physical flow of work, material, or documentation. It's crucial to observe the work at the Gemba to get an accurate map. Measure the steps taken in a process, multiply by the number of workdays, and you'll see how much waste can be eliminated with simple changes like better organization (6S) or a high quality cart.

A spaghetti map should be quick and dirty, not a polished document. It should become outdated within weeks as improvements are made. Color-coding different processes can also help visualize where the most significant inefficiencies lie.

Value Stream Mapping

A value stream map (VSM) captures all critical flows in a process, including value-added and non-value-added activities. It shows production control, suppliers, customers, communication, and transportation lines. The focus should be on the bottom of the map, which details the basic process flow, cycle times, changeover times, uptime, and inventory between processes.

The goal is to reduce work-in-progress (WIP) and scheduled work-in-progress (SWIP) inventory between processes. As you reduce WIP, you'll expose process problems, allowing for targeted improvements.

By understanding and implementing these process mapping techniques, you can significantly improve efficiency, reduce waste, and streamline workflows in your organization.

CHAPTER 4

Root Cause Analysis

I drove up to Minnesota to a plastics company to meet with the supervisor and the two top leaders. We needed to tackle a quality improvement project because they had a product that was bowing out, making it hard for customers to install. We sat down to create a project charter, a crucial first step for any project.

I said, "Hey guys, we're going to have to figure out how to improve this." They admitted they didn't have any standard operating procedures (SOPs) and had no idea where to start. So, I suggested we do a simple fishbone diagram. Typically, we use the six M's, but I find it easier to start with the top five or six processes.

I drew a circle representing the perfect product, added a backbone, and drew five bones coming off it. I asked them to name their top processes, which I then labeled on each bone. Next, I added smaller bones for subprocesses. At the top, I explained the concept of a **C**ontrolled, **N**oise, or e**X**periment (CNX) assessment. The question process will go like this. Look at every process and ask, "Is it controlled, or is this noise?" If it does not have something controlling the process, like an SOP or a visual control, then it is noise, and you must create your control mechanism. Once you have developed controls for every process, then, and only then, you can do a "Controlled Scientific Experiment". This involves controlling every single factor to achieve high quality.

I used the analogy of bow hunting to explain. If you're trying to hit a target with no controls—changing your stance, erratic breathing, different shoes—you'll have a wide spread of hits. But if you control everything, you'll get a tight cluster near the target. Now, by making a minor adjustment, like breathing differently, you can hit the center. That's how you achieve high quality—by controlling your processes.

The Five Whys

The Five Whys technique is a simple but powerful tool for root cause analysis. However, be careful to focus on processes, not people. I once worked with an engineer who used the Five Whys to figure out why someone wasn't very bright. Needless to say, this approach doesn't make friends.

When doing a Five-Whys analysis, declare your intention. Otherwise, you'll come off as an annoying kid or a new employee who won't stop asking why. Let's say your toast is burnt. The first "why" might be, "It stayed in the toaster too long." This could split into "Timer set wrong" or "Timer malfunctioned." Another path could be "Too much heat," leading to "Heating element failure."

Breaking it down further, "Timer set wrong" might be due to "Read setting incorrectly," which could be because "Need glasses" or "Markings worn out." "Timer malfunctioned" could be due to "Loose connection" from "Kid dropped toaster on the floor." Each of these reveals actionable steps for improvement.

Cause and Effect Diagram

A cause and effect diagram, also known as a fishbone diagram, helps teams understand every process involved in a project. Start with the six M's: **M**an (people), **M**achine, **M**ethod, **M**aterial, **M**other Nature, and **M**easurement.

For example, let's say you have bad coffee. This is the circle at the end of your fishbone. The bones might include machines, manpower, methods, materials, mother nature, and measurement. Under manpower, you might list issues like rude staff, no training, or wrong coffee grounds. Under the method, you might list too much coffee, too much water, or no training. Under material, you could have wet packets, bad sugar, or ill-fitting lids.

Example of Fish-bone Diagram (Ishikawa diagram)

Example: Manufacturing   Define the Problem: Casting Product Cracking

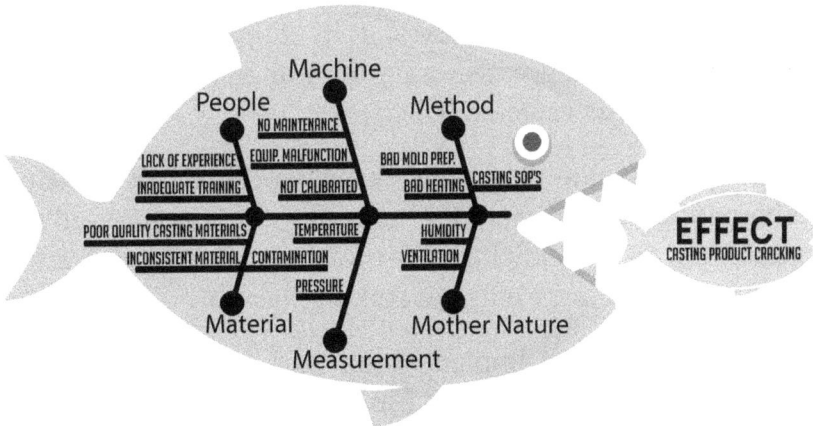

© Jerry Pykiet

However, I find it easier to simplify. Draw a circle for the perfect product, a backbone, and five or six bones for processes. Break down each process into steps, and you've started your SOP.

Conduct time studies on each process and create a playbook for different demand levels.

Examining the Waste

Each process step should be examined for excessive waste from the customer's perspective. There are three categories:

Value Added: Activities that change or transform material or information to meet customer requirements.

Non-Value Added but Necessary: Activities that don't add value but are necessary for the process, like documentation or inspections.

No Value Added: Activities that don't add value and waste time or resources, like walking or searching for tools.

On your process map or checklist, categorize each step as value-added, necessary but non-value-added, or no value-added. Use color coding for clarity. Typically, start by eliminating non-value-added steps, then reduce necessary but non-value-added steps, and finally optimize value-added steps.

For example, assume the welder is skilled. Focus on reducing or eliminating non-value-added steps like unnecessary walking or searching. By minimizing these wastes, you streamline the process, making it more efficient and productive.

By understanding and implementing root cause analysis and waste assessment techniques, you can significantly improve quality, reduce inefficiencies, and streamline processes in your organization.

CHAPTER 5

Ride the W.A.V.E.

When I started working at Chad's Weld Shop, which is in the oilfield business, the shop was in disarray. The 12,000-square-foot space housed 33 welders, and the walls, about three to four feet deep, were cluttered with junk, tools, and parts. To eliminate waste and keep the welders within their beachfront area, three feet, three seconds away from the blue light when they're welding—we made 33 custom quarter-inch thick metal carts.

Each cart reflected the welder's personality. One cart looked like an off-road Jeep for someone who loved Jeeps, while another had handlebars, exhaust pipes, and saddlebags for a Harley enthusiast. We even had carts designed to look like guitars for music lovers. This personalization made work more enjoyable and allowed them to put their personality into their workspace, something most employers wouldn't allow.

By the end, nothing unnecessary was left on the walls. Essential items like torches or ladders were securely mounted, and each cart had a specific parking spot. One welder even added a coffee maker to his cart so he'd have a fresh pot of coffee ready every morning. They all enjoyed "riding the W.A.V.E."

<u>W</u>aste <u>A</u>nd <u>V</u>ariation <u>E</u>limination - Riding the W.A.V.E

The acronym for Waste and Variation Elimination is "DOWN TIME," representing the eight elements of a waste-free enterprise (eight ways to show respect):

Defects

Overproduction

Waiting

Non-Value Added Process Steps (Overprocessing)

Transportation

Inventory

Motion

Employee Underutilization

Defects

Defects are determined by the process's customer. If something drives the customer crazy, it's a defect. Most defects are caused by broken processes, not people. This requires a cultural shift, especially in places with a gangster-like leadership style that blames individuals rather than the broken process that is designed to allow the defects to happen.

To achieve a defect-free process, use poka-yoke (mistake-proofing). After a defect is created, say, "Let's poka-yoke this," to make the process foolproof. We will discuss poka-yoke more in the book. Poka-yoke is key to quality.

Overproduction

Overproduction means producing too much inventory before it's actually needed, which ends up taking up valuable space. Or taking up too much space, which is a natural human behavior. You know there's waste when you see piles of inventory stacked up between value-added process steps. It starts to look like a log jam when you start looking for inventory taking up too much space. Some people might think it's smart to pile up inventory as a form of insurance, but it often just slows everything down and takes too much time to find defects.

Imagine playing "Tetris" with your facility layout to minimize waste. This can really help streamline operations and open extra space for new opportunities. A practical approach is to use caution tape to section off the extra space you have created. Otherwise, it will fill back up with inventory and you will lose your gains. You could even suggest to the owner that this space might be better used for expanding the business.

When you produce more than what's needed, you tie up resources, clutter the workspace, and increase your cycle time. This makes it harder to find and access the items that are actually needed. Plus, it can lead to a lot of unnecessary handling and movement, which wastes time and effort.

To address overproduction, it's important to match production closely with demand. This means producing just enough to meet customer needs without creating excess inventory. By doing so, you can free up space and resources that could be used more effectively elsewhere.

One way to achieve this is by implementing LEAN manufacturing principles. This involves continuously assessing and adjusting your production processes to eliminate waste and improve efficiency. For example, you can use tools like Kanban systems (Visual minimum and maximum of inventory) to manage inventory levels and ensure that production is closely aligned with demand.

Another effective strategy is to involve employees in identifying and addressing overproduction issues. They're often the ones who see the day-to-day impacts of overproduction and can provide valuable insights into how to reduce waste. Encouraging a culture of incremental continuous improvement can lead to more effective and sustainable solutions.

Overproduction is a common issue that can significantly impact the efficiency and effectiveness of a business. By taking steps to minimize overproduction and align production with demand, you can reduce waste, free up valuable resources, and create a more streamlined and efficient operation. Remember, sometimes less is more. By focusing on producing just what is needed, you can create a more responsive and agile business that is better equipped to meet the needs of your customers.

Waiting

Waiting involves any delays for people, machines, methods, inspections, information, customers, or inventory. Think about it—picture actual humans as your inventory and they are waiting impatiently. That gives you a clear idea of the impact.

If you've got excessive WIP (work in process), it just sits there, waiting for all the other parts to be worked on. It's like being stuck in line at Disneyland. You're excited about getting on the ride, but you must wait for everyone else first.

Waiting is a huge waste in any process. It's not just about physical waiting; it's also about lost opportunities and wasted time. When machines aren't running, or employees aren't working because they're waiting for the next step, productivity takes a hit.

One key way to tackle waiting is to identify where these delays are happening. Are machines idle because they're waiting for maintenance? Are employees standing around because they're waiting for instructions or materials? Are customers left waiting because the product isn't ready? Each of these scenarios highlights a gap in the process that needs fixing.

To address waiting, you need to streamline processes and improve coordination. This might mean better scheduling to ensure that materials and information are available when needed. It could also involve cross-training employees so they can switch tasks and keep things moving even when there's a delay in one area.

Another effective strategy is to implement visual management systems. These systems make it easy to see where work is flowing smoothly and where it's getting stuck. For example, using Kanban boards can help track task progress and identify bottlenecks in real time.

It's also crucial to foster a culture of incremental continuous improvement. Encourage everyone in the organization to look for ways to reduce waiting times. Small adjustments can add up to significant improvements. Maybe it's rearranging the workspace to minimize movement or adjusting work schedules to better align with production needs.

Involving employees in the process is vital. They're the ones on the front lines and often have the best insights into where delays occur and how to fix them. Regularly solicit their feedback and involve them in problem-solving efforts.

In conclusion, waiting is more than just an inconvenience—it's a major drain on productivity and efficiency. By identifying and addressing the causes of waiting, you can create a smoother, more efficient process that benefits everyone. Imagine your operations running like a well-oiled machine, with minimal delays and maximum productivity. That's the goal we're aiming to obtain.

Non-Value-Added Process Steps (Overprocessing)

Non-value-added steps involve steps that the customer isn't paying for. Think about it from the customer's perspective. They aren't paying for searching or walking, so it's crucial to reduce or eliminate these whenever possible. This is a key part of LEAN or continuous improvement practices.

When we talk about non-value-added steps, we're referring to all those extra steps that don't directly contribute to what the customer values. These steps can be a major source of waste in any process.

To tackle this, the first step is to map out your entire process (process map it). Take a close look at each step and ask yourself, "Does this add value from the customer's perspective?" If the answer is no, then it's time to reconsider whether that step is necessary.

For example, extensive documentation might seem important, but if it doesn't add value for the customer, it's just adding extra work and slowing things down. Similarly, grinding welds to perfection might not be necessary if the customer doesn't require such a high level of finish. By questioning these practices, we can find ways to shorten our processes.

Implementing lean principles means constantly looking for ways to improve and eliminate waste. One effective approach is to involve everyone in the organization in this effort. Encourage employees to identify non-value-added activities in their daily work and suggest improvements. Often, those closest to the process have the best insights into where inefficiencies lie.

Another strategy is to use tools like Value Stream Mapping (VSM). This helps visualize the entire process and pinpoint areas where non-value-added activities occur. By focusing on these areas, you can make targeted improvements that significantly impact overall efficiency.

Incremental Continuous Improvement is about making small, incremental changes that add up to big results over time.

It's not about making drastic changes all at once but rather about consistently seeking out and implementing incremental improvements. This mindset helps create a culture where productivity and creating value are always top priorities.

Reducing non-value-added processing is essential for improving efficiency and delivering better value to customers. By closely examining each step in the process and eliminating those that don't add value, we can streamline operations and focus on what really matters. Remember, the goal is to make the process as minimum as possible while still meeting the customers' needs and expectations. Let's commit to identifying and eliminating waste, one step at a time, to achieve incremental continuous improvement and world-class operational excellence.

Transportation

Transportation waste is any movement outside your beachfront property. Use a spaghetti map and time study to identify and minimize transportation waste. Ideally, processes should be as close to each other as possible.

Transportation waste is the unnecessary movement of materials, products, or information throughout a process. This type of waste can lead to increased lead times, higher costs, and potential damage to goods, people, and equipment.

Key aspects include:

1. **Unnecessary Movement:** Moving items that don't need to be moved, such as transporting materials between distant locations within a facility.

2. **Distance:** Long distances between workstations or storage areas can slow down processes and increase handling time.

3. Handling: Excessive handling of materials can lead to wear and tear or damage, impacting quality.

To reduce transportation waste, organizations can optimize layout, improve process flows, and implement just-in-time inventory systems. These systems help minimize unnecessary movement and improve production.

Inventory

Inventory is the root cause of ALL waste.

Excess inventory is a clear sign that your operations lack perfect flow. When you have too much inventory, resources are being tied up unnecessarily, which can slow down your process and take up valuable space. To keep things running smoothly, inventory should be visually controlled using color codes, lines, labels, signs, and standard operating procedures (SOPs). Implementing these tools helps everyone understand where things belong and how much of each item should be on hand.

One effective method to manage inventory is through a Kanban system. This system sets minimum and maximum inventory levels to ensure you have just enough to meet demand without overstocking. When inventory levels drop below the minimum, it signals that it's time to reorder. Conversely, having a maximum limit prevents overproduction and excess storage.

But inventory isn't just about physical products. Even air can be considered inventory. For example, in a fruit company with different temperature-controlled rooms, you must measure how often doors open and the cost of maintaining those temperatures. Every time a door opens, the cold air escapes, and the cooling system must work harder to maintain the desired temperature. This extra effort translates into higher energy costs and potential inefficiencies.

To tackle excess inventory, start by analyzing your current stock levels and identifying items that are overstocked. Ask yourself why these items are piling up. Is it due to inaccurate demand forecasting, long lead times, or perhaps a lack of proper storage management? By pinpointing the root cause, you can take targeted actions to reduce excess inventory.

Additionally, consider the flow of materials through your facility. Are there bottlenecks that cause delays and lead to inventory buildup? Streamlining the flow of materials can help reduce waiting times and improve overall efficiency. This might involve rearranging the layout of your workspace, optimizing storage locations, or even adjusting your production schedule to better match demand.

Implementing a first-in, first-out (FIFO) system can also help manage inventory more effectively. By ensuring that older inventory is used before newer stock, you can prevent items from becoming obsolete or expiring. This approach is particularly important for perishable goods, where freshness is key to maintaining quality.

Another strategy is to regularly review and update your inventory management practices. This includes conducting periodic audits to ensure that inventory levels are accurate and aligned with actual usage. Make sure the team members closest to the inventory own the tracking process.

Managing inventory effectively is crucial for maintaining a smooth and efficient operation. By implementing visual controls, using a Kanban system, and regularly reviewing your practices, you can minimize excess inventory and create a more streamlined process. Remember, every bit of inventory represents tied-up resources and potential waste. By focusing on inventory management, you can free up these resources and improve your overall efficiency.

Motion

Motion waste refers to unnecessary movement within the beachfront property. Every extra step or reach outside your ergonomic zone to the process is considered motion waste. It might seem trivial, but over time, these unnecessary movements can add up and lead to significant inefficiencies.

One effective tool for identifying and reducing motion waste is a spaghetti map. This visual representation of the flow of movements helps pinpoint areas where excessive motion occurs. By mapping out the paths taken by people, materials, and equipment, you can clearly see where improvements are needed.

The goal is to stay within your "Bruce Lee motion zone." This means focusing on smooth, efficient movements without bending down or reaching high. Think about it like martial arts—Bruce Lee was known for his precise and smooth movements. In the same way, minimizing unnecessary motion in your work area can boost efficiency and reduce fatigue.

Consider the layout of your workspace. Are frequently used items within easy reach? Is there a clear and direct path between workstations? By arranging tools, materials, and equipment logically and ergonomically, you can reduce the need for excessive movement.

For example, if you're constantly bending down to pick up tools from a lower shelf, it might be time to rearrange your storage. Place commonly used items at waist height, where they are easily accessible without strain. Similarly, avoid placing frequently used tools or materials on high shelves that require stretching to reach.

In addition to physical layout changes, consider the workflow itself. Are there steps in your process that require unnecessary movement? Can tasks be reorganized to minimize back-and-forth trips? Sometimes, small adjustments in the sequence of operations can lead to significant reductions in motion waste.

Another important aspect is the use of appropriate equipment. For instance, using carts with scissor lifts or trolleys to transport materials can reduce the need for carrying heavy loads over long distances. Similarly, using adjustable-height workbenches or carts can help maintain a comfortable and efficient working posture.

Training and awareness also play a crucial role in reducing motion waste. Encourage employees to be mindful of their movements and look for ways to improve efficiency. Small habits, like positioning tools within easy reach before starting a task, can make a big difference over time.

Minimizing motion waste is all about making work smoother and more efficient. By using tools like spaghetti maps and staying within your "Bruce Lee motion zone", you can identify areas for improvement and implement changes that reduce unnecessary movement. These adjustments not only enhance productivity but also create a more comfortable and ergonomic work environment. Let's focus on making every movement count and transforming our workspace into a model of efficiency. Like the Navy says, "Slow is smooth, and smooth is fast."

Employee Underutilization

Employees are gold mines for improvement ideas. It's crucial to create a collaborative environment where everyone feels encouraged to share their thoughts and suggestions. Think of it like gold mining, you must sort through a lot of mud, rock, and permafrost to find those valuable nuggets of wisdom. Research shows that only about 50% of the ideas are going to be of no value, 25% are going to be neutral, and the last 25% is pure gold. If I were a gold miner and you told me not to mine a particular mine because only every 4th shovel load is pure gold, I would say you are crazy, and I would start filling my SUV with all the mud, rock, permafrost, and pure gold as fast as I could. The key is to sift through all the suggestions and identify those with the potential to make a real difference.

When you tap into your employees' potential, you unlock a wealth of insights that can drive meaningful improvements. Encouraging a culture of open communication and collaboration not only empowers employees but also fosters innovation. It's all about creating an atmosphere where everyone feels their ideas are valued and worth sharing.

Start by setting up regular brainstorming sessions or suggestion boxes where employees can freely contribute their ideas. (Note: an untrained workforce will give poor ideas) Make it clear that no idea is too small or insignificant. Sometimes, the most groundbreaking improvements come from the simplest suggestions.

Once you've gathered a pool of ideas, it's important to evaluate them carefully. Look for those that align with your business goals and have the potential for significant impact. Prioritize these ideas and develop a plan to implement them. It's also essential to provide feedback to employees on the status of their suggestions, letting them know which ideas are being pursued and why.

Involving employees in the implementation process can further enhance the success of improvement projects. When people see their ideas being put into action, it boosts morale and reinforces the value of their contributions. It also encourages them to continue thinking creatively and sharing their thoughts.

To maximize the benefits of employee ideas, consider providing training on problem-solving and incremental continuous improvement techniques. This equips employees with the skills to identify issues and develop effective solutions. By investing in their development, you create a more capable and proactive workforce.

Celebrating successes is another important aspect. When an employee's idea leads to a positive change, acknowledge their contribution publicly. This not only rewards the individual but also inspires others to come forward with their suggestions.

Employees are an invaluable resource for driving improvement and innovation. By fostering a culture of collaboration and actively seeking out their ideas, you can uncover hidden gems that lead to significant enhancements in your business. Remember, even though only a portion of the ideas may have a substantial impact, those that do are incredibly valuable. Let's commit to mining the gold within our teams and leveraging their insights to propel our business forward.

Waste Assessment

Waste is any activity that doesn't directly add value from the customer's perspective. In order to identify and eliminate waste, it's crucial to categorize activities into three main groups: value-added, no value but needed, and no value at all.

Value-added activities are those that the customer is willing to pay for. These are the essential tasks that directly contribute to creating the product or service the customer desires. For example, in a manufacturing process, assembling parts to create a finished product is a value-added activity.

On the other hand, some activities don't add direct value but are necessary for the process to function. These are categorized as "no value but needed." Think of tasks like equipment maintenance or quality inspections. While the customer might not pay specifically for these activities, they are essential to ensure the product meets quality standards and the process runs smoothly.

The final category, "no value at all," includes activities that are pure waste. These tasks don't contribute to the product or service in any meaningful way and should be eliminated. Examples might include excessive material movement, waiting times, or redundant paperwork.

To assess waste effectively, start by mapping out your entire process. Look at each step critically and ask, "Does this add value from the customer's perspective?" If the answer is no, determine whether the activity is necessary for the process or if it can be eliminated.

Visual tools like process maps or value stream maps can be incredibly helpful. These tools provide a clear visual representation of the workflow, making it easier to spot inefficiencies and areas of waste. By seeing the process laid out step-by-step, you can identify which activities fall into each of the three categories.

Once you've identified wasteful activities, the next step is to develop a plan to address them. For value-added activities, focus on optimizing and streamlining them to maximize efficiency. For activities that are of no value but needed, look for ways to reduce their impact. For instance, you could schedule regular maintenance to prevent unexpected breakdowns or implement quality control measures that reduce the need for extensive inspections.

Eliminating activities that add no value at all can have a significant impact on overall efficiency. This might involve reorganizing the workspace to reduce unnecessary movement, implementing better scheduling to minimize waiting times, or digitizing paperwork to eliminate redundant processes.

Engaging employees in the waste assessment process is also crucial. They often have first-hand knowledge of where inefficiencies lie and can provide valuable insights into potential improvements. Encourage a culture of incremental continuous improvement where everyone is empowered to identify and suggest ways to reduce waste.

Waste assessment is a fundamental step in improving efficiency and delivering better value to customers. By categorizing activities into value-added, no value but needed, and no value at all, you can focus on optimizing your processes and eliminating waste. This not only enhances productivity but also creates a more streamlined and effective operation. Let's commit to regularly assessing and addressing waste to ensure we're always delivering the best possible value to our customers.

Examples:

> Moving: If you constantly move inventory, it's waste. But if you're a moving company, it's value-added.

> Maintaining Records: Usually no value but needed, so minimize it.

> Setup Changeover: Often no value but needed, so reduce it with quick changeover projects.

> Polishing: Ask the customer how shiny they want the product. This can reduce polishing time by 95-98%.

> Grinding: Usually, no value at all or no value but needed, depending on the customer's requirements.

The point is to always talk to the customer to determine what adds value.

Understanding and eliminating waste and variation can significantly improve your processes, making them more efficient and customer-focused. By riding the W.A.V.E., you can create a more productive and enjoyable work environment.

CHAPTER 6

Lay It Out to Flow

I was working at a factory in the middle of North Carolina, where they built beams with lifters. The welding shop that welded the beams together was on one side of the facility, while the assembly shop that installed the winders, cables, and lifting equipment was on the completely opposite side. Within the cells, things flowed well, but they were batching between the welding shop and the assembly shop. If the lifting beams were logs, then we would have a big logjam between departments. It's ok to have one or two logs but any more than two would be creating waste.

We decided to put the assembly in the weld shop without increasing their footprint and fit everything needed into that space. By eliminating all the waste, we realized we could fit a lot in a small area. We put everything on carts and divided the weld shop workflow so that every welder would finish in 30 minutes and then pass their cart to the next welder. Then, we split the assembly shop into three cells all totaling 30 minutes per lift. This change allowed us to produce a brand-new finished lifter every 30 minutes, compared to the previous time of one and a half to two hours.

In the end, the team members who had to work in that area loved the project because they worked less, got paid the same or more, and went home with more energy. This improved their quality of life both at work and at home with their families.

Principles of Workplace Layout

Creating an efficient and ergonomic workplace layout is essential for maximizing productivity and minimizing strain.

Here are nine key principles to guide you:

Principle 1: Keep Motion to a Minimum

Try to have everything you need right in front of you. This reduces unnecessary movement and helps you work more efficiently. Imagine having all your tools and materials within arm's reach, so you don't have to waste time searching for them. By arranging your workspace this way, you can focus on the task at hand without constant interruptions. Try to stay in your beachfront property, three feet, three seconds from the point of use.

Principle 2: Use Gravity Instead of Muscles

Whenever possible, let gravity do the heavy lifting. Tools like Flex Pipe can be incredibly helpful. Flex Pipe systems work like an adult version of an erector set, allowing you to build custom structures that make it easier to move heavy items with minimal effort. By utilizing gravity and smart tools, you reduce the physical strain on your body, making your work environment safer and more efficient. Flex Pipe can engineer a cart system that links with your inbound and or outbound so you will never have to lift a bin again. It is a dream come true for ICI lovers.

Principle 3: Avoid Zig-Zagging Motions

Quick directional changes can be both inefficient and tiring. Aim to move in straight, smooth lines whenever possible. This not only speeds up your workflow but also reduces the risk of injuries from sudden, awkward movements. Think of your movements as a smooth dance, avoiding any unnecessary zigzagging.

Principle 4: Move with a Steady Rhythm

Consistency is key. Move like a metronome, keeping a steady rhythm as you work. This principle is like being in a band where everyone plays in sync. By maintaining a consistent pace, you avoid burnout and maintain productivity throughout the day. It's all about finding a rhythm that allows you to work efficiently without rushing or dragging. Try playing music while you work. It is a good idea to rotate music channels daily so that everyone gets to listen to their music.

Principle 5: Keep Materials Close and In Front

Consider this your beachfront property. The items you use most frequently should be kept close and directly in front of you. This prime real estate within your workspace ensures you can grab what you need quickly and easily, minimizing wasted time and effort. By organizing your materials this way, you create a more streamlined and effective workflow.

Principle 6: Arrange Materials and Tools in Order of Use

Organize your workspace so that materials and tools are arranged in the order you'll use them. This logical sequence helps you work more efficiently and prevents you from constantly reaching over or around items to get what you need. It's like setting up an assembly line where each step flows naturally into the next.

Principle 7: Work at the Proper Ergonomic Height

Ensure that your work surface is at the correct height for ergonomic comfort. Typically, this means having your workspace at a height where your elbows are at a 90-degree angle. Working at the right height reduces strain on your back, shoulders, and arms, preventing fatigue and injury.

Principle 8: Locate Materials So They Are Easy to Lift

Place materials and tools at heights that are easy to reach without excessive bending or stretching. Nothing should be too low or too high. Items used frequently should be stored at waist height or slightly above to minimize the need for awkward lifting.

Principle 9: Place Keyboards at the Correct Height

If you work at a computer, ensure that your keyboard is at the correct height to promote ergonomic typing. Use ergonomic typing aids if necessary. Your keyboard should be positioned so that your wrists remain straight, and your hands are at or slightly below elbow level. This helps prevent repetitive strain injuries like carpal tunnel syndrome.

To optimize your workspace, use a spaghetti diagram to see the flow and layout of your current setup. This visual tool helps you track movements and identify inefficiencies. Once you have a clear picture, create an ideal spaghetti map to visualize and form ideas for a new, more efficient layout. By comparing your current setup to the ideal, you can pinpoint specific changes that will reduce unnecessary movement and improve overall workflow.

Little's Law

Little's Law describes the relationship between WIP (work in process), process cycle time (PCT), and throughput. The formula is:

Cycle Time = WIP / Throughput

For example, if you have six items and your throughput is two items per day, your cycle time is three days. This fundamental relationship applies to any process and helps size people, paperwork, projects, and processes.

Lower process cycle time equals more learning cycles, which means more opportunities to learn about the process and create mastery skills.

Example: Disneyland

In March:
WIP = 5 people
Exit rate = 1 person per minute
Cycle time = 5 minutes

In July:
WIP = 13 people
Exit rate = 1 person per minute
Cycle time = 13 minutes

A fixed capacity exit rate with increased people (WIP) equals slower process cycle times. We practice Little's Law every time we choose a checkout line at the grocery store.

Time Trap vs. Constraint

Let's say we're making dessert cookies. We have our input and the following operations:

Operation 1: 30 seconds

Operation 2: 40 seconds

Operation 3: 45 seconds

Operation 4: 35 seconds

The time trap is the operation with the largest cycle time, which is Operation 3 at 45 seconds. If customer demand is 75 units per hour, we need to determine if it's a time trap or a constraint.

Calculate:

60 minutes × 60 seconds = 3600 seconds

Then:

3600 seconds / 45 seconds = 80 units per hour

If demand is 75 units per hour, it's a time trap. If demand is 85 units per hour, it's a constraint and time for an improvement project.

Traditional Batching vs. Continuous Flow

At a factory in Florida, we aimed for continuous flow. We found five cranes hidden on a rack and learned they were making extra inventory and pushing it onto the assemblers. We designed the process for one beam at a time, so welders would stop working and go help down the line or work on a plan B project if they completed a beam and the scheduled work-in-process (SWIP) parking spot still had a cart in it that held one beam.

Traditional batching builds up large amounts of WIP as insurance against machine downtime and all the other hidden problems. Continuous flow is more fragile but makes team members more valuable and requires careful planning and scheduling.

Results of Batching:

Excess WIP

Lots of waiting

Excessive conveyance

Excessive movement

No flexibility

Results of Continuous Flow:

Reduced WIP

Flexibility in the cell

Customer controls production based on demand

Supports quality at the source

Creates an enjoyable team atmosphere

One Piece Flow

Think of loggers from the 1800s. If everyone puts their logs in front of yours, creating a log jam, you lose profit. In a perfect one-piece flow, each log goes straight to the customer without stopping.

Scheduled WIP (SWIP) involves having indicators to pull products into the next process. Once a parking spot is full, workers may help others or work on continuous improvement projects.

Benefits of Continuous Flow:

Reduces cycle time

Identifies defects faster

Increases flexibility

Customer-driven production

Reducing WIP and Finding Boulders

Imagine your process as a boat going across the deep waters, with WIP being the deep water. As you strive to reduce your WIP or water level, you will start to expose many boulders (time traps, rework, defects, waste, running out of consumables, and more). You will have to get your scuba diving gear on and chisel down (ICI) the boulders that pop up as they appear. Reducing WIP slowly helps identify and address these issues before they become major problems. At Toyota, they gradually reduced WIP, creating a more efficient process. It's crucial to create a fun environment during this challenging process to reduce stress.

CHAPTER 7

Visual Controls in the Cabinet Shop

I worked at a cabinet shop in Oklahoma that started with about eight to ten team members. Before I moved on, the team had grown to over 50 members in just over two years. It was an exciting journey.

One thing we discovered was the power of a visual workplace, also known as a visual factory. We realized we could run the shop using big floor stickers. We had a 56-inch-wide printer that could print images like wrapped cars. Most of the team members didn't speak English, so we turned to emojis. Everyone understands facial expressions, so I showed them a menu of emojis, and we selected ones that would help us control the carts.

The purpose of creating flow in a factory is to control your WIP (work-in-process) or scheduled WIP. We kept no more than four carts of cabinet parts between each value-add location.

The first parking spot for a cart had an emoji of a house on fire with smoke and hands in the air, looking really scared. The second spot had an emoji of a house on fire but less freaked out. The third spot had an emoji of a house starting to smoke, looking concerned. The fourth spot had a very happy house emoji, indicating everything was okay.

This system worked because if the fourth spot was empty, you'd see the two-foot by five-foot sticker and know it was okay. If the third spot was empty, you'd see the concerned house emoji, indicating you should start getting worried and make sure to fill that spot. If the second spot was empty, the house emoji started showing fire, and you should start moving the filled cart into that parking spot to put the fire out. Now, if you saw the fourth parking spot was empty, and the house was completely on fire and freaked-out arms wailing about, it meant extreme problems—there were no carts to pull from.

We implemented this visual control system throughout the entire cabinet shop, creating perfect flow with a visual que emoji system or visual controls.

Visual Controls

Visual controls quickly communicate status or provide feedback about performance relative to goals. They keep teams focused on their objectives and processes, outline tool and equipment locations, set daily targets, and illustrate tasks.

Examples of Visual Controls:

Safety Signs: Warn about hot areas, hard hat zones, and PPE requirements.

Kanban: Visuals for minimum and maximum inventory levels, using color codes like red for low inventory, yellow for warning, and green for good levels. You can also use a two-bin system. Fill each bin with what you use each day, and when one runs out, put it in a refill Kanban bin area and have the backup bin slide forward. This will allow you to have a scheduled refill time at the beginning or end of each day.

Goals and Checklists: Success boards display maps of audited areas, checklists, and targets.

Shadow Boards: Outline tools on a shadow board or 6S foam boards, using drastic colors for easy visual inspection.

Color Coding: Use ULINE or 3M tape, 6S foam boards, paint pens, metal-solvent dye, and 3D Puff Paint to color-code tools and equipment. Every value-added location should have its own color. If you run out of colors, start mixing them like black and yellow or red and white.

Communication Boards: Show performance metrics, past 6S audit scores, a before-and-after picture, realistic expectations, and real-time status hour-by-hour tracking with digital clocks. Always add your company logo to make it look professional.

Red Tag Zones: Designated red tables for unidentified or misplaced items, cleaned out regularly to reduce decision-making for team members.

Visual controls should be of high quality to communicate the importance of continuous improvement and the value of the people in the area. These controls dramatically reduce or eliminate defects and the need for work-related discussions, allowing for more personal interactions and relationship building.

Invest time and resources into creating high-quality visual controls. They should be clear, easy to understand, and durable. This investment shows the importance of continuous improvement and respect for the team.

Implementing effective visual controls creates a more efficient, safe, and enjoyable work environment. These controls help maintain focus, improve communication, and ensure that everyone knows their role and responsibilities within the workflow.

CHAPTER 8

Inspecting the Defects Out

I was working at one of the largest weld wire factories in the country, processing massive 1,200-1,300 pound spools of welding wire. During a Green Belt course I was teaching, I conducted an exercise to highlight the challenges of inspection. I had about seven lab professionals, all experienced inspectors in lab coats, count the number of F's in two sentences within a box on a PowerPoint slide.

The sentences read: "Count the number of F's within the box. Finished files are the result of years of scientific study, combined with the experience of years". Despite their experience", not one of them got the correct number of F's (8). This demonstrated that we cannot rely solely on inspection to ensure the quality of our parts.

Then I had them count the E's in another sentence: "Count the number of E's within the box. Each Easter, every exiled Englishman entertains endless entreaties for exotic eggs." Again, they struggled, and about half missed some E's (21). This exercise showed that even seasoned professionals could miss errors, proving the importance of mistake-proofing processes.

Mistake-Proof Everything

Another example is the game of telephone. In a process with five people, even with a 95% yield rate, the final message can be significantly distorted. At 99% accuracy, you still lose 5% of the message, which can be critical in business. Small improvements in yield can lead to enormous productivity gains and cost reductions.

Inspection Methods

There are several types of inspection methods:

Traditional Inspection: An inspection guru at the end of the line checks products, sorting good from bad. This method reduces problems before customers see them but doesn't prevent defects from occurring.

Statistical Sampling: Lab techs take small samples and test them. This reduces inspection costs but doesn't prevent defects from reaching customers. Feedback is often too slow to be effective.

Successive Checks: Each process inspects the previous one. While 100% of the work is inspected, it's costly and can still allow defects to reach the customer.

Full Inspection: When defects are high, everyone inspects everything. This doesn't prevent defects but finds problems before they exit the process. It's costly and slow, often seen in administrative tasks where data flow is critical.

Inspection adds cost without adding value. Customers are not paying for inspections. The only reason we have inspections is because the process is designed to allow defects to happen. Would you pay more for a Ford truck if they said it was inspected 500 more times? The one with the 500 more inspections costs $5,000 more than all the other trucks on the lot. What truck would you want?

CHAPTER 9

Mistake Proofing

I was working at a pneumatics company that supplied the parts for dump truck hydraulics to go up and down. This company was one of the biggest suppliers in the world, with five or six big buildings. Each building had its own culture, depending on the leader. Most had great cultures with respect for people and minimal waste. But one building had a "wild animal" of a leader, creating a chaotic environment.

In this building, a worker kept running a forklift into the lights, breaking the large pole lights and causing a big mess. The supervisor would yell and embarrass the worker in front of everyone, adding to the chaos. I walked in one day, feeling like I was entering the Wild West, expecting gunslingers to appear.

After the supervisor calmed down, I suggested a poka-yoke (mistake-proofing) solution. We needed to design the process to prevent this defect from happening again. We painted a line on the lift, indicating where to stop to avoid hitting the lights. This worked for a while, but a few months later, the worker hit the lights again.

Remembering our conversation, the supervisor realized it wasn't the worker's fault but a broken process. He fabricated a jig that physically stopped the forklift from reaching the lights, and we never had that issue again.

Foundations of Poka-Yoke

Poka-yoke is Japanese for "mistake-proofing." It's all about designing mechanisms and processes that stop defects or make defects obvious at a glance. The concept is simple but incredibly powerful, and it can transform the way we approach quality control and process improvement.

We have poka-yokes all around us. Think about when you make coffee in the morning. You pour the water into the back of the coffee maker, and if you overfill it with coffee, there is a little hole at the top of the water tank that will let the extra water out. It is a lot better to have clean water run over your countertop than steaming hot coffee that can stain your countertops. When I was growing up, we had safety sensors on the riding lawn mower, so if you jumped off the mower, it would shut off. We see them when we fill up with gas, turn on our turn signals, and even back up with our backup cameras and sensors all around our cars.

Here are key points to Poka-Yoke:

First, a poka-yoke device prevents mistakes or makes them obvious. These devices are designed to catch errors before they become defects. For example, a simple fixture that only allows parts to be assembled in the correct orientation can prevent assembly errors. Another example is a sensor that alerts workers if a component is missing, ensuring that the final product is complete and functional.

Preventing mistakes is crucial because defects result from errors in imperfect processes. Every process, no matter how well-designed, has the potential for human error. Poka-yoke aims to eliminate these errors by adding checks and safeguards that make it almost impossible to make a mistake. By addressing the root causes of defects, we can significantly improve product quality and consistency.

Defects occur either because we're unaware of errors or fail to correct them in time. Sometimes, errors are so subtle that they go unnoticed until it's too late. Other times, we might spot an error but don't have a quick and effective way to correct it. Poka-yoke helps by making errors more visible and providing immediate feedback so corrections can be made on the spot.

Defects are major customer dissatisfiers and create hidden costs for producers. When customers receive defective products, it not only damages their trust but also leads to returns, repairs, and replacements—all of which are costly for producers. Beyond these direct costs, there are also hidden costs like lost reputation and potential future sales. By implementing poka-yoke, we can reduce these risks and ensure a higher level of customer satisfaction.

Let's consider some practical examples of poka-yoke in action. In a manufacturing setting, a color-coded system might be used to ensure that the correct parts are used at each stage of assembly. If a part doesn't match the expected color, it's an immediate indication that something is wrong. In an office environment, poka-yoke can be as simple as standardized forms that guide users to fill in all required fields, reducing the chance of missing critical information.

Another example is the use of jigs and fixtures that hold components in the correct position during machining or assembly. These tools not only speed up the process but also ensure precision and consistency, effectively eliminating errors caused by misalignment or improper handling.

In software development, poka-yoke can be seen in features like auto-save and error alerts. Auto-save prevents data loss by regularly saving progress, while error alerts notify users when an action could lead to a mistake, such as closing a document without saving changes.

Implementing poka-yoke doesn't have to be expensive or complex. Often, the simplest solutions are the most effective. The key is to focus on understanding the process and identifying points where errors are likely to occur. From there, we can brainstorm ways to make mistakes either impossible or immediately noticeable.

The foundations of poka-yoke lie in its ability to prevent mistakes and make errors obvious. By integrating these principles into our processes, we can significantly reduce defects, enhance quality, and improve customer satisfaction. It's about creating an environment where doing things right the first time becomes the norm. Let's embrace poka-yoke and build systems that not only catch mistakes but also prevent them from happening in the first place. By doing so, we can ensure our products and services meet the highest standards of quality and reliability.

Poka-Yoke Detection Systems

There are two types of poka-yoke detection systems: the control warning approach and the prevention approach.

Control Warning Approach

This approach shuts down the process or signals personnel when an error occurs. It keeps suspect work in place when the process step is incomplete and stops the process when an irregularity is detected. This method is useful if mistake-proofing is too costly to implement but still aims for zero defects.

Example: A system won't let a customer order if their information doesn't match the master database. Imagine ordering flowers online. In the early days, if you entered one wrong digit on your credit card, your order would go through, but no flowers would be delivered. Now, the system instantly tells you if your card information is incorrect, allowing you to fix it immediately and ensure timely delivery.

Prevention Approach

This method prevents errors from being produced, achieving 100% elimination of mistakes and zero defects.

Example:

Autofill customer information from the master database into order form fields. I once worked in an administrative office in Oklahoma, where people manually retyped Excel sheets into new forms, causing a lot of unnecessary work. We switched to a master database to eliminate this waste and prevent errors.

Your ability to mistake-proof a process is only limited by your imagination. As Shigeo Shingo, a pioneer in the field, once said, "The best approach is to assume that defects will happen and create processes that won't allow them".

By embracing poka-yoke and continuously improving processes, we can significantly reduce defects and enhance overall quality. This not only improves customer satisfaction but also simplifies operations, making work more efficient and enjoyable for everyone involved. Remember, installing good poka-yoke systems is the only way to achieve close to 100% quality at work and in your personal life.

CHAPTER 10

Auditing for Success

I was working at a recycling company when we started noticing that we were losing the gains we had made through our success program. I got together with the leadership team and suggested we start auditing each area at the beginning or end of every month and giving them scores. At first, this made everyone uncomfortable. But I had a great Vice President who made sure all the leaders showed up for the auditing meetings.

We developed a 6S audit checklist based on each part of the 6S and used it to audit each area. We gave them scores, where each point was a "bad" score, like in golf—you want as few points as possible. We called them "not-yet points." For every item out of place, they got a point, up to five points per topic. The auditor would note what they saw, and that would go into the area's corrective action or incremental continuous improvement plan. They had to fix everything on the audit by the next month.

We kept these audit forms visible in each area all month long. Initially, some area owners were biased, so we made the person being audited hold the clipboard and document the information. Everyone else would find the good and bad things about the area, turning it into an Easter egg hunt.

Out of over 20 areas, seven or eight would get perfect scores each month. After a year, even trivial defects, like not having a home for an eraser, were found and fixed. The owner incentivized this by offering $50 to everyone with a perfect score and giving a traveling trophy to the person who completed the most action items and had a perfect score.

This traveling trophy became a big deal. Each area created high-quality homes for the trophy, like inserts in walls with LED lights and custom laser-cut metal logos, or glass cases. If an area didn't win, the empty glass case was a clear reminder. This was a significant investment for the owner, but he realized sustainment is just as challenging as building the success program. It improved team morale and was well worth it.

Standard Work

Standard work defines how people interact with their working environment, including machines, computers, and other tools, to produce or process a product or service. It ensures tasks are performed consistently and efficiently, maintaining a high standard of quality.

Standard work outlines the motion of the operator and the sequence to the machines, creating a prescribed, repeating series of operations assigned to a single team member. This sequence is balanced to takt time or slightly faster, about 95% of takt. By clearly defining each step, it ensures every operator performs the task the same way, minimizing variability and increasing efficiency. For instance, in a manufacturing setting, if an operator needs to assemble a product, standard work will specify the exact steps they need to follow. This might include the order in which parts are picked, the tools used, and the precise movements to be made. This reduces unnecessary actions and streamlines the workflow.

Documenting processes and assumptions made is crucial for maintaining consistency. This includes detailing why certain steps are performed in a particular way and the conditions under which the process operates. Documentation is essential for maintaining a stable and predictable workflow, especially when training new employees or when changes to the process are needed. For example, if a certain temperature is required for a machine to operate efficiently, this assumption should be documented. This way, anyone can understand the rationale behind the procedure and follow it accurately.

Standard work also serves as a standard operating procedure and a training aid for new workers. It provides a clear, step-by-step guide on how to perform tasks, making it easier for new employees to learn quickly and accurately. This reduces the learning curve and helps maintain productivity even as new team members are brought on board. When a new worker starts, they can refer to the standard work documentation to understand their responsibilities and the exact way to carry out their tasks. This consistency ensures that quality and efficiency are maintained.

Establishing the relationship between takt time and cycle time is another critical aspect of standard work. Takt time is the rate at which a product needs to be completed to meet customer demand, while cycle time is the actual time it takes to complete a task. Standard work helps ensure these times are aligned, so production meets demand without overproducing or underproducing. For example, if the takt time is 60 seconds, the cycle time should be around 57 seconds (95% of takt) to ensure a smooth flow of operations without creating bottlenecks or idle time.

Including critical elements in standard work is essential for guiding the production process. These elements provide a comprehensive framework that ensures all necessary steps are followed and there is a clear understanding of the workflow. Knowing the takt time helps in planning the production schedule effectively, while understanding the work sequence ensures that every step is performed in the correct order, minimizing errors and rework.

Standard work is a fundamental aspect of any efficient and high-quality production process. By detailing motion and sequence, documenting processes and assumptions, providing training aids, establishing the relationship between takt time and cycle time, and including critical elements, standard work ensures consistency, efficiency, and quality. Embracing these principles helps create a more streamlined and productive working environment, benefiting both the organization and its employees.

Purpose and Requirements

The purpose of standard work is to ensure that work and expectations are safe, efficient, and consistent. This foundation is crucial for maintaining high standards and achieving long-term success. Here are the three main requirements:

First, safety is paramount. The work environment and procedures must prioritize the safety of all team members. This means implementing measures that prevent accidents and injuries, providing proper training, and ensuring that everyone follows safety protocols. A safe workplace not only protects employees but also boosts morale and productivity.

Next, quality is essential. Consistent processes ensure high-quality output and reduce defects. When everyone follows the same standard procedures, it minimizes variability and errors, leading to a more reliable and superior product or service. This consistency is key to meeting customer expectations and building a strong reputation.

Efficiency is also critical. Streamlined operations reduce waste and increase productivity. By eliminating unnecessary steps and optimizing workflows, we can accomplish tasks more quickly and with fewer resources. This not only improves the bottom line but also allows us to respond more swiftly to customer demands and market changes.

Implementing standard work involves creating detailed procedures for each task, ensuring that everyone knows exactly what to do and how to do it. This clarity helps prevent misunderstandings and mistakes. Regular audits are necessary to maintain these standards. By periodically reviewing and updating our processes, we can identify areas for improvement and ensure that we continue to operate at peak efficiency.

These sustainment tools are vital for creating a consistent, safe, and efficient work environment. They help ensure that the gains achieved through our success program are maintained over the long term. Regular audits and updates keep us on track, allowing us to adapt to new challenges and opportunities without sacrificing our core principles.

For example, in a manufacturing setting, standard work might involve specific guidelines for operating machinery, handling materials, and assembling products. Each step is documented and reviewed regularly to ensure compliance and identify potential improvements. Safety checks, quality controls, and efficiency measures are all integrated into the standard work process, creating a comprehensive approach to excellence.

In the office, standard work can apply to tasks such as data entry, customer service, and project management. Clear procedures and regular training help employees perform their duties accurately and efficiently. By standardizing these processes, we can reduce errors, improve customer satisfaction, and increase overall productivity.

The benefits of standard work extend beyond individual tasks. By fostering a culture of continuous improvement, we encourage everyone to contribute ideas for making our processes better. This collaborative approach not only enhances our operations but also empowers employees, giving them a sense of ownership and pride in their work.

The purpose of standard work is to create a safe, efficient, and consistent work environment. By focusing on safety, quality, and efficiency, we can achieve high standards and sustain them over time. Regular audits and updates ensure that we continue to improve and adapt, maintaining the gains achieved through our success program. This commitment to excellence benefits both our team and our customers, driving long-term success and satisfaction.

As we reach the end of this exploration into the intricacies of creating a world-class culture and improving processes, it's crucial to reflect on the journey and the lessons we've learned. The principles and strategies we've discussed are more than just theoretical concepts; they are practical tools that can transform any organization.

Creating a world-class culture is not an overnight endeavor. It's a continuous process that requires dedication, commitment, and a willingness to adapt. At the heart of this transformation is the understanding that culture is the foundation upon which all successful strategies are built. As Peter Drucker famously said earlier in the book, "Culture eats strategy for breakfast". This statement underscores the importance of fostering a positive, engaging, and motivating environment where employees feel valued and respected.

One of the key elements in building such a culture is the emphasis on safety, quality, and efficiency. Safety must always be the top priority. A safe work environment not only protects employees but also enhances their morale and productivity. Quality, on the other hand, ensures that the products or services meet or exceed customer expectations. Consistent, high-quality output is achieved through well-defined processes and standard work procedures. Efficiency, achieved by streamlining operations and eliminating waste, allows organizations to do more with less, thereby increasing profitability and competitiveness.

The role of leadership in this cultural transformation cannot be overstated. Leaders set the tone and lead by example. They must embody the values and behaviors they wish to see in their teams. This means being approachable, open to feedback, and committed to continuous improvement. By fostering an environment of trust and transparency, leaders can encourage employees to share their ideas and insights, which are invaluable for driving innovation and improvement.

Standard work is another crucial component of this journey. It defines the interaction between people and their working environment, ensuring that tasks are performed consistently and efficiently. By detailing motion and sequence, documenting processes and assumptions, and providing training aids, standard work helps create a stable foundation for continuous improvement. It also establishes the relationship between takt time and cycle time, which is essential for maintaining a smooth and efficient workflow.

Regular audits and updates are necessary to maintain these standards and ensure that the gains achieved through the success program are sustained over time. These audits help identify areas for improvement and ensure that processes remain aligned with organizational goals. They also provide an opportunity to recognize and celebrate successes, which can boost morale and reinforce the importance of continuous improvement.

One of the most powerful tools for driving continuous improvement is the concept of poka-yoke or mistake-proofing. By designing processes and systems that prevent errors or make them immediately obvious, organizations can significantly reduce defects and improve quality. This proactive approach to quality control not only enhances customer satisfaction but also reduces the costs associated with rework and waste.

Employee involvement is another critical factor in the success of any improvement initiative. Employees are on the front lines and often have the best insights into where inefficiencies lie and how they can be addressed. By creating a collaborative environment where employees feel encouraged to share their ideas and suggestions, organizations can tap into a wealth of knowledge and creativity. Regular brainstorming sessions, suggestion boxes, and open forums can all help foster this culture of collaboration and innovation.

Visual controls are another effective strategy for maintaining focus and improving communication. By providing clear, easily understood visual cues, organizations can quickly communicate status, goals, and expectations. This helps keep teams aligned and focused on their objectives, reducing the need for constant supervision and allowing for more autonomy and empowerment.

As we conclude this journey, it's important to remember that the path to a world-class culture and continuous improvement is ongoing. There will always be new challenges to face and new opportunities to seize. By staying committed to the principles of safety, quality, and efficiency, and by fostering a culture of trust, transparency, and continuous improvement, organizations can achieve sustained success and create a workplace where everyone thrives.

The journey to creating a world-class culture and improving processes is multifaceted and requires a holistic approach to get one percent better every day.

It involves not only implementing practical tools and strategies but also fostering an environment where employees feel valued and empowered. By focusing on safety, quality, efficiency, leadership, standard work, continuous improvement, employee involvement, and visual controls, organizations can transform their operations and achieve long-term success. This commitment to excellence benefits everyone involved, from the employees who feel motivated and engaged to the customers who receive high-quality products and services. Let's embrace this journey and strive to continuously improve, innovate, and create a workplace that we can all be proud of.

Finding projects can be challenging, especially if you are looking for a project that saves time, increases quality and safety, and helps create the perfect plant tour. Continuously getting ready for the ideal plant tour is essential. We should always be prepared for our top customers to walk through our offices and shops. It is more fun when you are always ready to show off your team's accomplishments.

To be a good project spotter, you want to think of yourself as a crime scene investigator—like those shows on TV with fancy cars and see-through lit-up whiteboards. The crime that has been committed is waste and variation in your processes and what you pass on to your internal customers. We want to ride the W.A.V.E. of improvement (Waste and Variation Elimination).

We pull out our old trusty crime-scene investigation tool book and start with the 8 wastes. I like to call it the 8 ways to show respect to yourself, your team members, and your internal customers. Your internal customer is the person you give your products to in the shop or send data to in the office.

Now that you have your investigation tool, you can get started. You want to observe the crime of waste and variation, live. Start by observing what drives people the craziest, takes up the most time, or creates the most defects. Now, put on your investigation hat and start observing. Take pictures of everything in scope. If it's an office process, start snipping away.

Then, you would want to do a spaghetti map or a process map to get the current condition. If it's an office process, it will be a process map; if you're improving your environment, it will be a spaghetti map. Get at least six or seven-time studies. Now that you have enough data to get started, put all your data on the wall and look for waste and variation.

Time to spot the 8 wastes. Some investigation time... Find your D.O.W.N - T.I.M.E.

- **Defects:** The customer of the process determines the defect. Poka-Yoke!

- **Over Production:** Too much inventory between processes. Too much space.

- **Waiting:** Person, machines, method, inspection, information, customers, inventory, and more are all waiting for better flow.

- **Non-Value-Add Processing:** Steps that the customer is not paying for.

- **Transportation:** Any movement outside of your beachfront property.

- **Inventory:** Inventory is the root cause of all waste. Everything is inventory.

- **Motion:** Movement within the beachfront property. Spaghetti map it.

- **E**mployee Underutilization: Employees are gold mines for improvement ideas.

Be the change you want to see first, and then teach others. Most importantly, this is designed for you and your team members to have fun and create memorable experiences together.

Life is short, let's live it together.

Your friend,
Jerry Pykiet

Author Bio

Jerry Pykiet is a seasoned expert in business innovation and process improvement. He is the founder of Blue Brook Consulting Inc., which has been in business for more than 15 years. The company has helped over a hundred businesses build continuous improvement programs while certifying thousands in LEAN Six Sigma (LSS) with Yellow, Green, and Black Belt Certifications.

With decades of experience, Jerry has dedicated his career to helping organizations build continuous improvement programs that have connected organizations across the country. His last CI Program, which he built, connected a holding firm's companies from Minnesota, North Carolina, Florida, and many facilities in between. They all managed their ICIs (1% better) from one website and one database, utilizing Power BI to generate graphs distributed weekly to all facility team members.

Jerry has a degree in Marketing and Business Management with a focus on International Business. He is a LEAN Six Sigma Black Belt and a certified Front-Line Leader Coach. Jerry's dedication to his community is exemplified by his four-year tenure serving as an elected city commissioner, teaching kids through Junior Achievement and OK2 Grow and certifying veterans at night with Yellow Belts in LSS to help enhance their careers.

Jerry is married with three kids and lives in a small community outside of Tulsa. He married his high school sweetheart after spending too much time apart and enjoys camping and going to the lake with her every weekend. With two kids in their 20s and one getting ready to drive, he enjoys every minute at home.

Through his extensive knowledge and innovative approach to implementing continuous improvement, Jerry has helped numerous companies turn their ideas into rewarding, exciting, and profitable ventures. Whether aiming to generate revenue or reduce costs, his strategies have consistently delivered outstanding results.

Based in Tulsa, OK, Blue Brook Consulting partners with local universities and Tech Centers to provide world-class training in Lean Six Sigma and leadership.

www.ingramcontent.com/pod-product-compliance
Lightning Source LLC
Chambersburg PA
CBHW022014090426
42741CB00007B/1027